SARAH PALIN
political Rebel

by Nel Yomtov   illustrated by Francesca D'Ottavi

Consultant:
Richard Ellis, PhD
Mark O. Hatfield Professor of Politics
Willamette University
Salem, Oregon

CAPSTONE PRESS
a capstone imprint

Graphic Library is published by Capstone Press,
151 Good Counsel Drive, P.O. Box 669,
Mankato, Minnesota 56002.

www.capstonepub.com

Books published by Capstone Press are manufactured with paper containing at least 10 percent post-consumer waste.

Library of Congress Cataloging-in-Publication Data
Yomtov, Nelson.
Sarah Palin : political rebel / by Nel Yomtov ; illustrated by Francesca D'Ottavi.
p. cm.—(Graphic library. American graphic)
Includes bibliographical references and index.
Summary: "In graphic novel format, follows Sarah Palin during the 2008 presidential election campaign and details her subsequent involvement in politics and entertainment"—Provided by publisher.
ISBN 978-1-4296-6018-1 (library binding)
ISBN 978-1-4296-7341-9 (paperback)
1. Palin, Sarah, 1964- —Juvenile literature. 2. Governors—Alaska—Biography—Juvenile literature. 3. Vice-Presidential candidates—United States—Biography—Juvenile literature. 4. Presidents—United States—Election—2008—Juvenile literature. 5. Palin, Sarah, 1964- —Comic books, strips, etc. 6. Governors--Alaska--Biography—Comic books, strips, etc. 7. Vice-Presidential candidates—United States—Biography—Comic books, strips, etc. 8. Presidents—United States—Election—2008—Comic books, strips, etc. 9. Graphic novels. I. D'Ottavi, Francesca, ill. II. Title.
F910.7.P35Y66 2012
973.931092—dc22
[B] 2011001017

Printed in the United States of America in Stevens Point, Wisconsin.
032011 006111WZF11

Direct quotations appear in yellow on the following pages:

Pages 7, 8, 16 (first panel), and 19 (second panel) from *Game Change*, John Heilemann and Mark Halperin (New York: HarperCollins, 2010).

Pages 10 and 11 from "McCain and Palin in Dayton, Ohio," *The New York Times*, August 29, 2008.

Pages 14 and 15 from "Palin's Speech at the Republican National Convention," *The New York Times*, September 3, 2008.

Page 16 (second panel) from "One-On-One with Sarah Palin," *CBS News*, September 24, 2008.

Page 17 (second panel) from *The Battle for America 2008*, Dan Balz and Haynes Johnson (New York: Viking, 2009).

Page 17 (third panel) from "Transcript of Palin, Biden Debate," *CNN*, October 2, 2008.

Page 18 (first panel) from "Palin Hits Obama for 'Terrorist' Connection," CNN, October 4, 2008.

Page 18 (second panel) from "The Wright Stuff," *The New York Times*, October 5, 2008.

Page 18 (third panel) from "Heels On, Gloves Off, Palin Says," *The Los Angeles Times*, October 5, 2008.

Page 19 (first panel) from "Palin on Michigan Pullout: 'I Want to Try,'" *CBS News*, October 3, 2008.

Page 21 from "Tina Fey as Sarah Palin Nails it Again on 'Saturday Night Live' Debate Skit," *Chicago Sun-Times*, October 4, 2008.

Page 23 from *Going Rogue: An American Life*, Sarah Palin, (New York: HarperCollins, 2009).

Page 25 from "Sarah Palin Resignation Speech," The Huffington Post, July 3, 2009.

Page 26 from "Sarah Palin's Keynote Speech at the National Tea Party Convention," *The Moderate Voice*, February 7, 2010.

Page 27 from video clip in "Sarah Palin's Alaska: Running for President on Reality TV?" *CNN*, November 16, 2010.

Page 29 from "Sarah Palin's Reagan Speech: 'Don't Tread on Me' Top Applause Lines Video," *Examiner.com*, February 5, 2011.

Art Director: Nathan Gassman

Editor: Christopher L. Harbo

Media Researcher: Wanda Winch

Production Specialist: Eric Manske

Photo Credits:
Dreamstime: Danwatt417, 29, Traceywood, 28 (Palin);
Shutterstock: skvoor (Alaska outline)

CHAPTER 1
THE OFFER 4

CHAPTER 2
A NEW POLITICAL VOICE 10

CHAPTER 3
THE VOTERS DECIDE 18

CHAPTER 4
NEW BEGINNINGS 24

SARAH FROM ALASKA 28
GLOSSARY 30
READ MORE 31
INTERNET SITES 31
INDEX 32

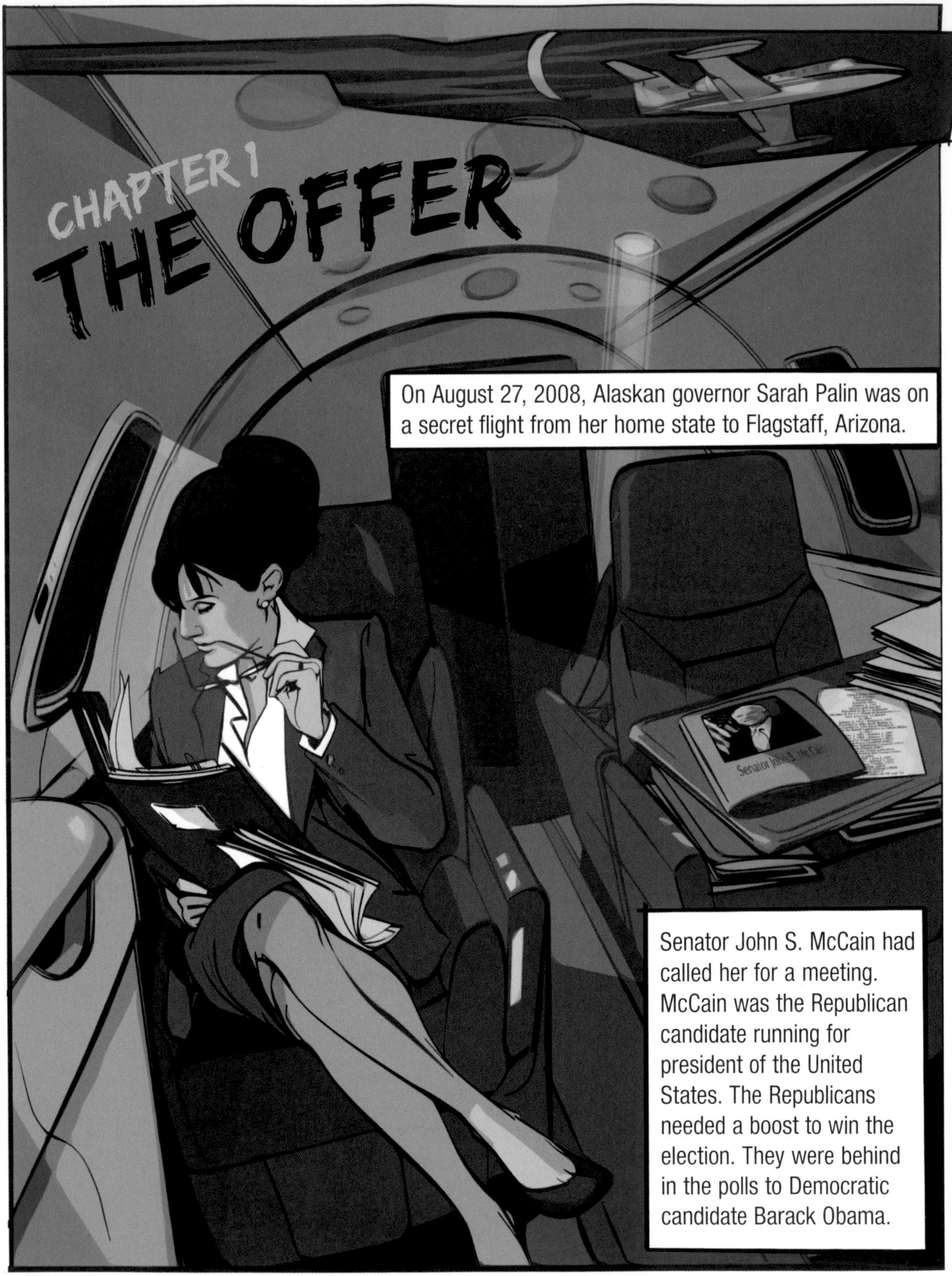
CHAPTER 1
THE OFFER
On August 27, 2008, Alaskan governor Sarah Palin was on a secret flight from her home state to Flagstaff, Arizona.
Senator John S. McCain had called her for a meeting. McCain was the Republican candidate running for president of the United States. The Republicans needed a boost to win the election. They were behind in the polls to Democratic candidate Barack Obama.

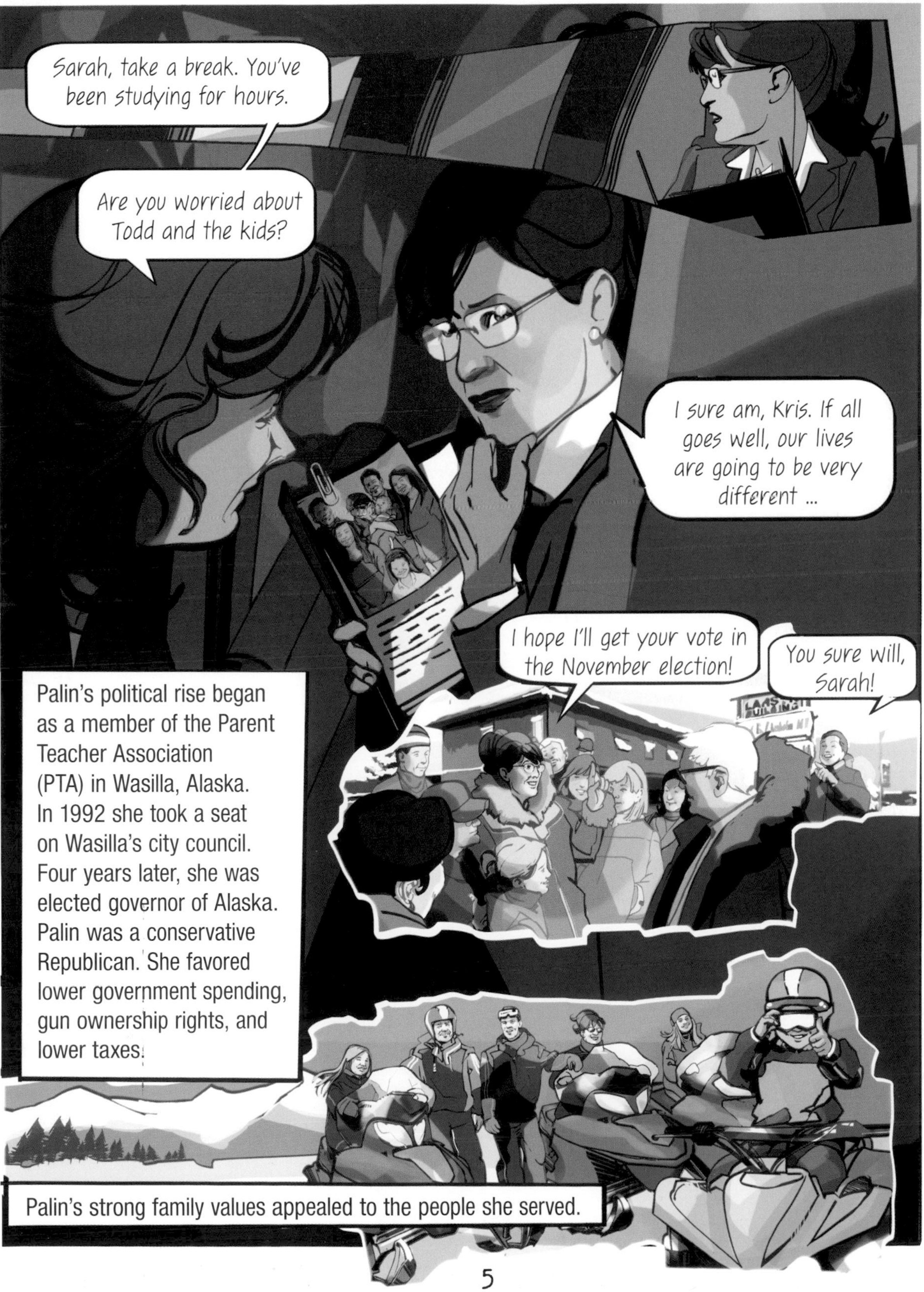
Sarah, take a break. You've been studying for hours.
Are you worried about Todd and the kids?
I sure am, Kris. If all goes well, our lives are going to be very different ...
I hope I'll get your vote in the November election!
You sure will, Sarah!
Palin's political rise began as a member of the Parent Teacher Association (PTA) in Wasilla, Alaska. In 1992 she took a seat on Wasilla's city council. Four years later, she was elected governor of Alaska. Palin was a conservative Republican. She favored lower government spending, gun ownership rights, and lower taxes.
Palin's strong family values appealed to the people she served.

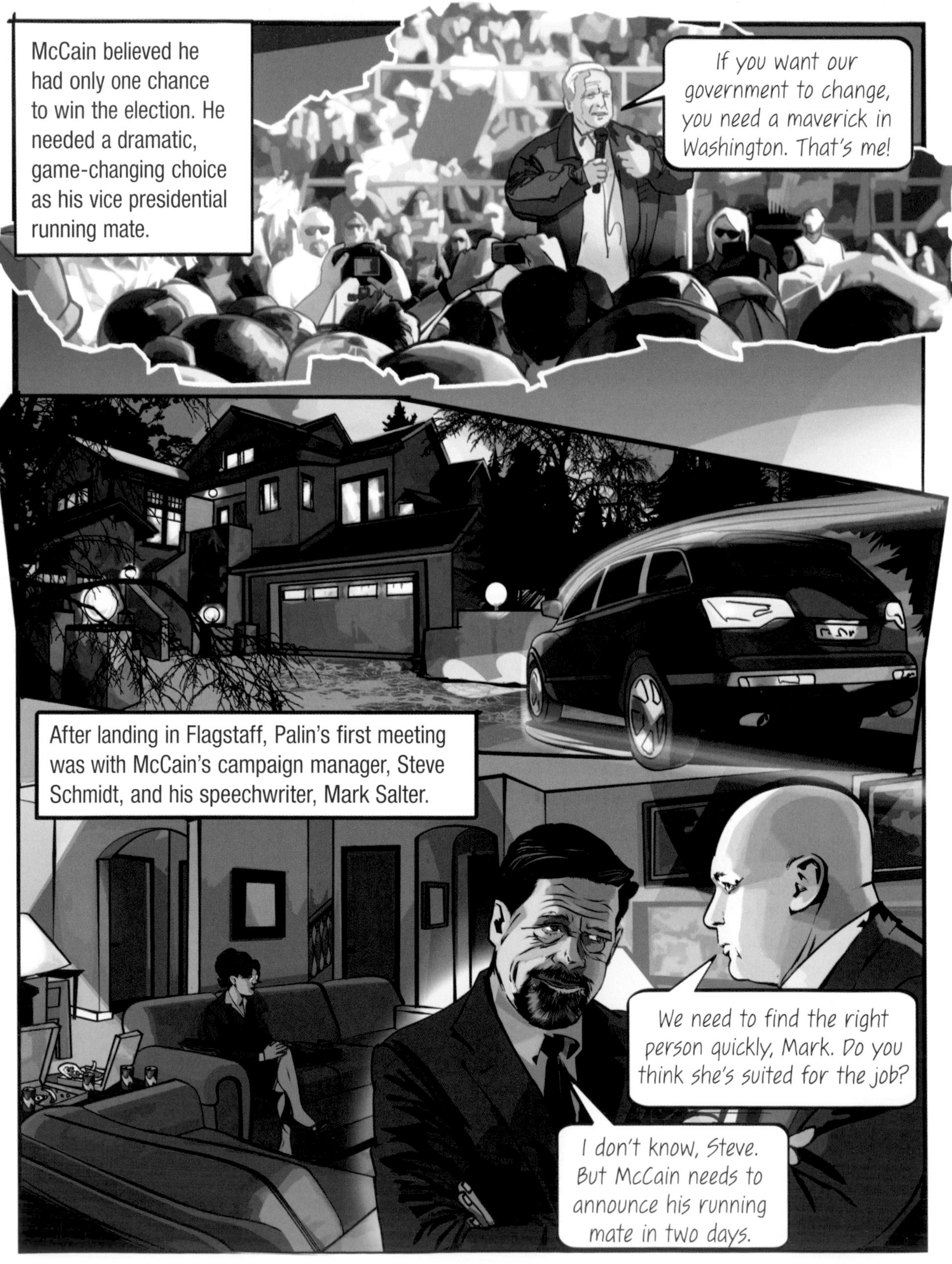
McCain believed he had only one chance to win the election. He needed a dramatic, game-changing choice as his vice presidential running mate.
If you want our government to change, you need a maverick in Washington. That's me!
After landing in Flagstaff, Palin's first meeting was with McCain's campaign manager, Steve Schmidt, and his speechwriter, Mark Salter.
We need to find the right person quickly, Mark. Do you think she's suited for the job?
I don't know, Steve. But McCain needs to announce his running mate in two days.

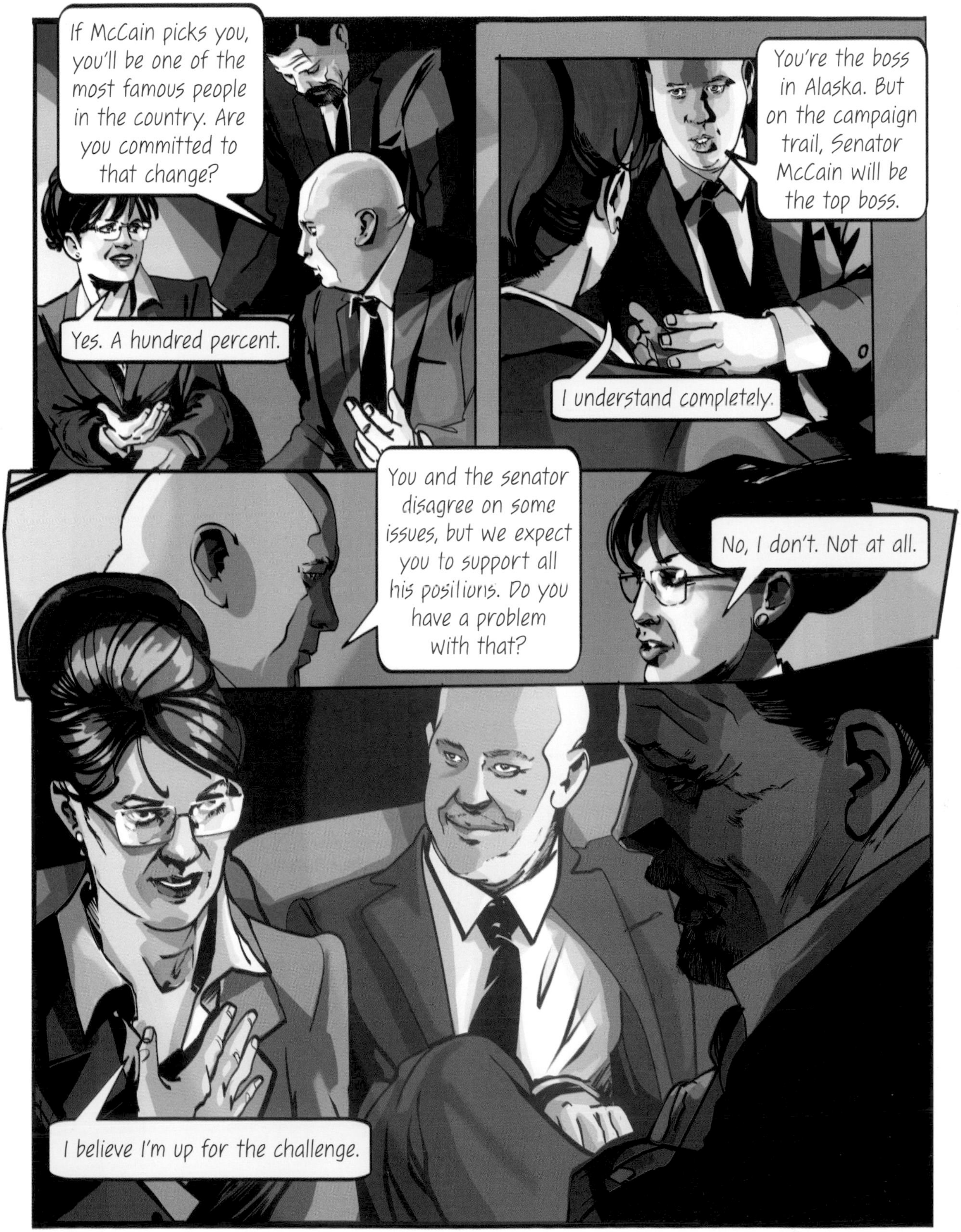
If McCain picks you, you'll be one of the most famous people in the country. Are you committed to that change?
Yes. A hundred percent.
You're the boss in Alaska. But on the campaign trail, Senator McCain will be the top boss.
I understand completely.
You and the senator disagree on some issues, but we expect you to support all his positions. Do you have a problem with that?
No, I don't. Not at all.
I believe I'm up for the challenge.

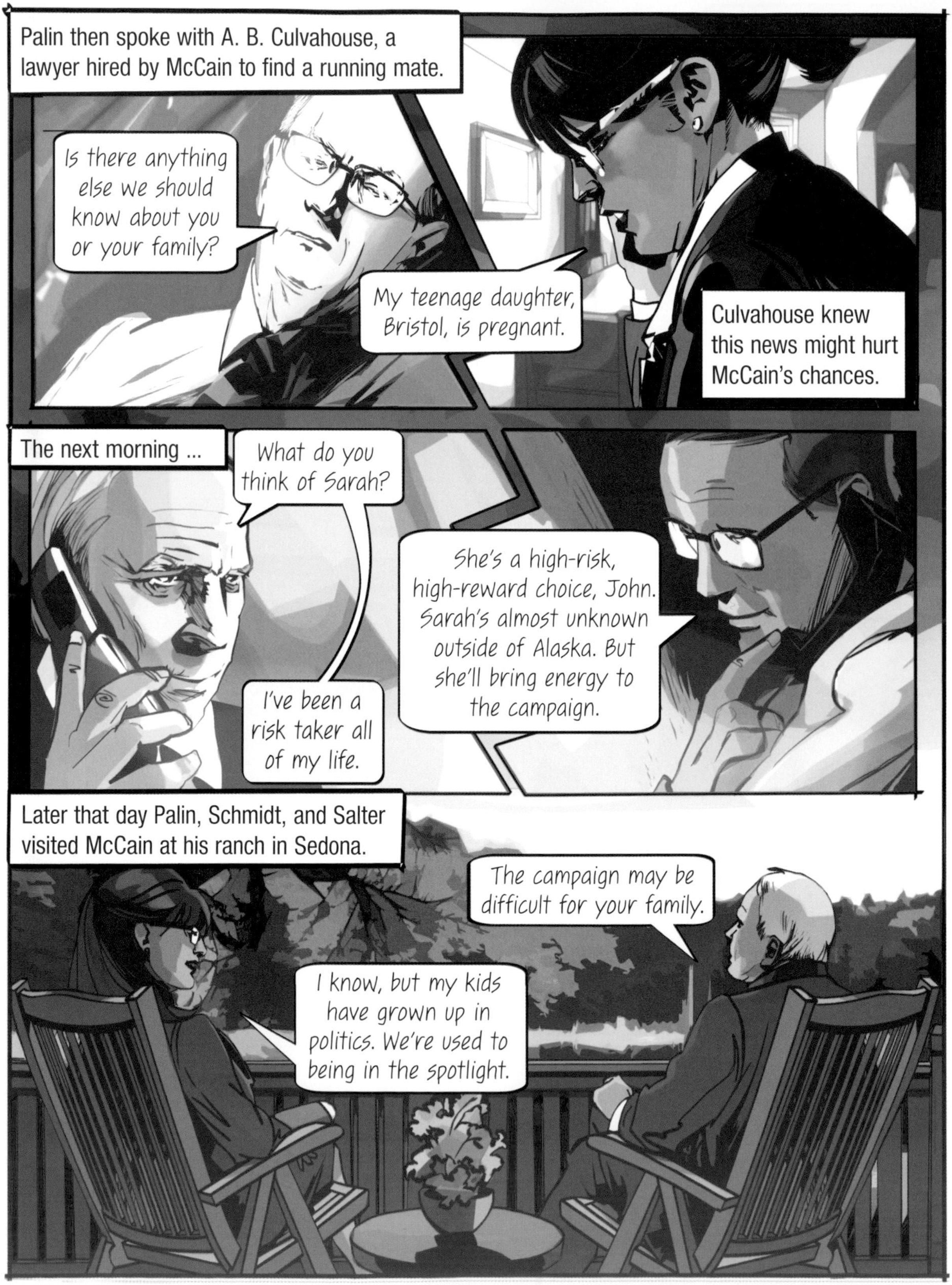
Palin then spoke with A. B. Culvahouse, a lawyer hired by McCain to find a running mate.
Is there anything else we should know about you or your family?
My teenage daughter, Bristol, is pregnant.
Culvahouse knew this news might hurt McCain's chances.
The next morning ...
What do you think of Sarah?
She's a high-risk, high-reward choice, John. Sarah's almost unknown outside of Alaska. But she'll bring energy to the campaign.
I've been a risk taker all of my life.
Later that day Palin, Schmidt, and Salter visited McCain at his ranch in Sedona.
The campaign may be difficult for your family.
I know, but my kids have grown up in politics. We're used to being in the spotlight.

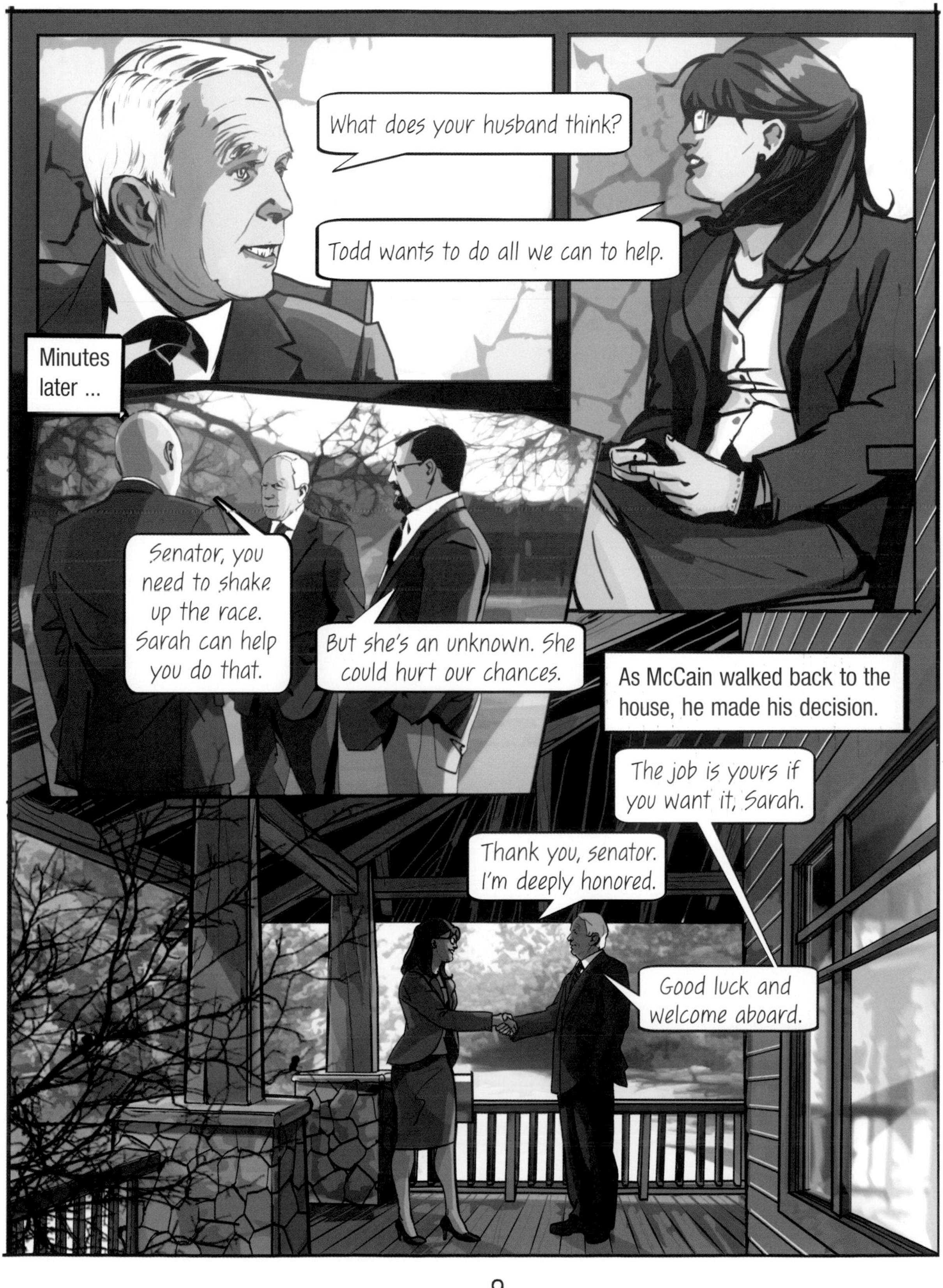
What does your husband think?
Todd wants to do all we can to help.
Minutes later ...
Senator, you need to shake up the race. Sarah can help you do that.
But she's an unknown. She could hurt our chances.
As McCain walked back to the house, he made his decision.
The job is yours if you want it, Sarah.
Thank you, senator. I'm deeply honored.
Good luck and welcome aboard.

CHAPTER 2
A NEW POLITICAL VOICE
On August 29, McCain introduced the first woman chosen for a Republican presidential ticket.
I found someone with an outstanding reputation ... someone who has stopped government from wasting taxpayers' money ...
COUNTRY FIRST
The person I'm about to introduce ... understands the problems, the hopes, and the values of working people ...
COUNTRY FIRST
I am very pleased and very privileged to introduce to you the next vice president of the United States—Governor Sarah Palin of the great state of Alaska!
I've gone from a small-town PTA member to vice presidential candidate. This can happen only in America!

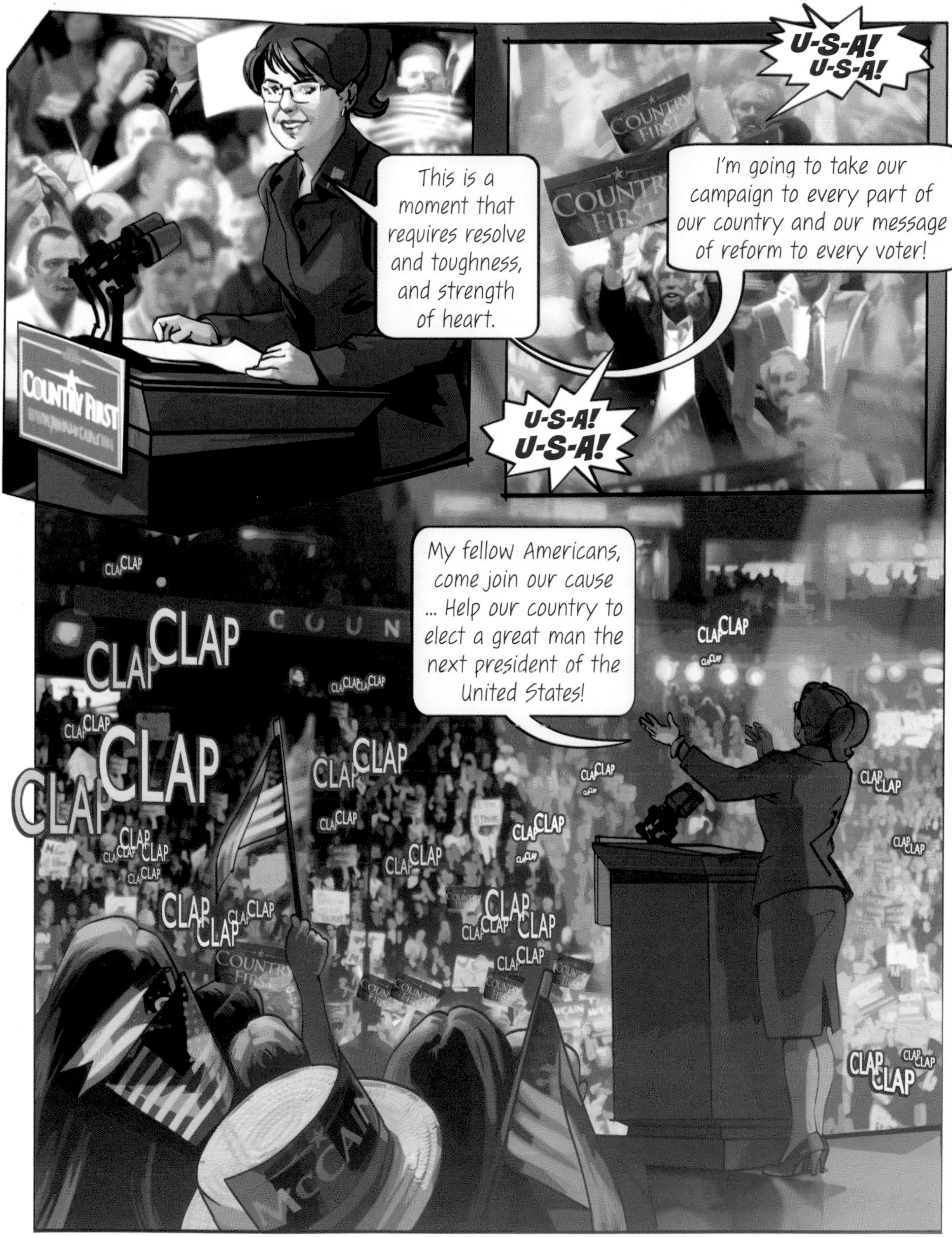
COUNTRY FIRST
This is a moment that requires resolve and toughness, and strength of heart.
U-S-A! U-S-A!
COUNTRY FIRST
I'm going to take our campaign to every part of our country and our message of reform to every voter!
U-S-A! U-S-A!
My fellow Americans, come join our cause ... Help our country to elect a great man the next president of the United States!
CLAP CLAP
CLAP CLAP
CLAP CLAP
CLAP CLAP
McCAIN

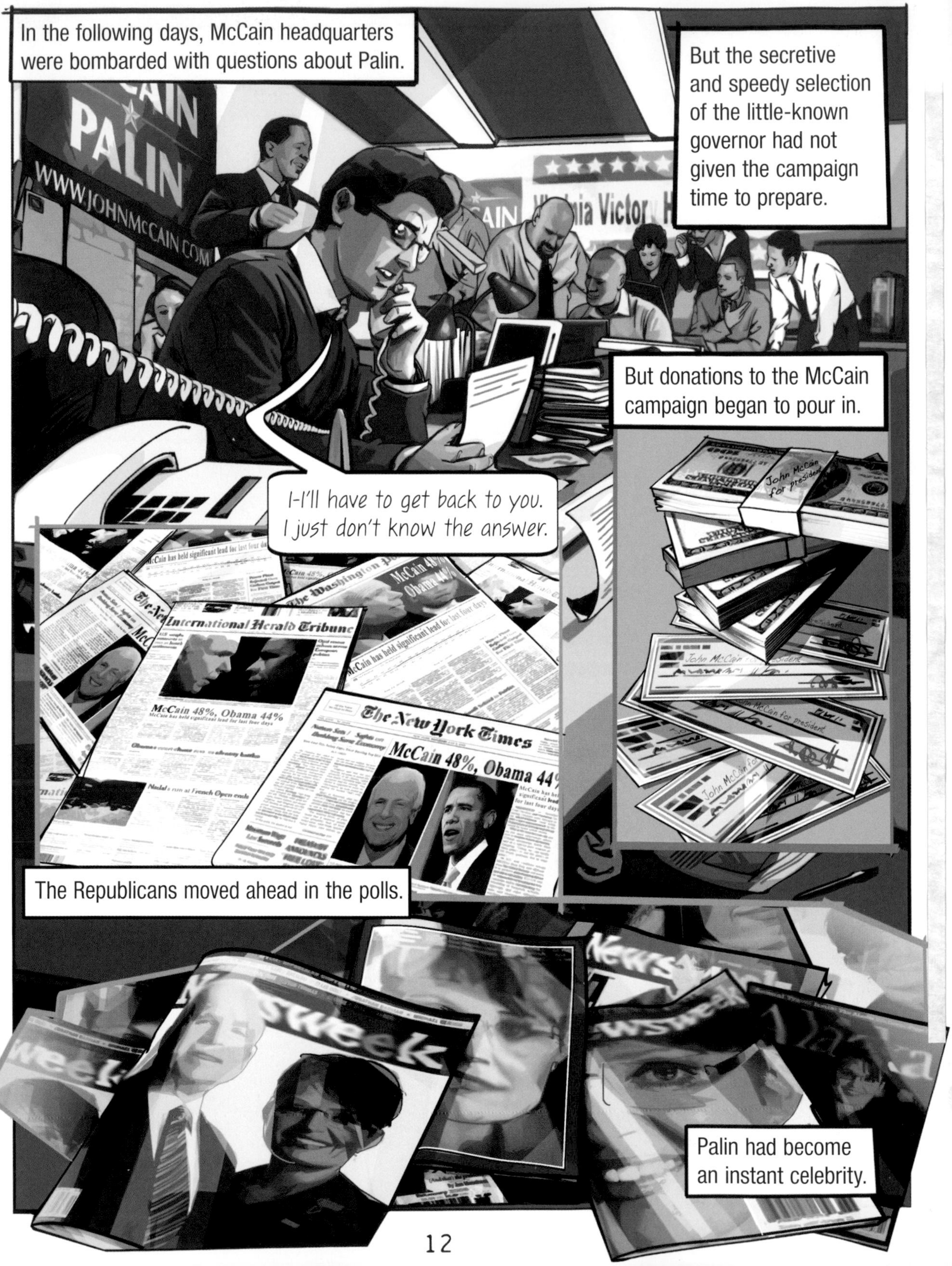
In the following days, McCain headquarters were bombarded with questions about Palin.
But the secretive and speedy selection of the little-known governor had not given the campaign time to prepare.
I-I'll have to get back to you. I just don't know the answer.
But donations to the McCain campaign began to pour in.
The Republicans moved ahead in the polls.
Palin had become an instant celebrity.

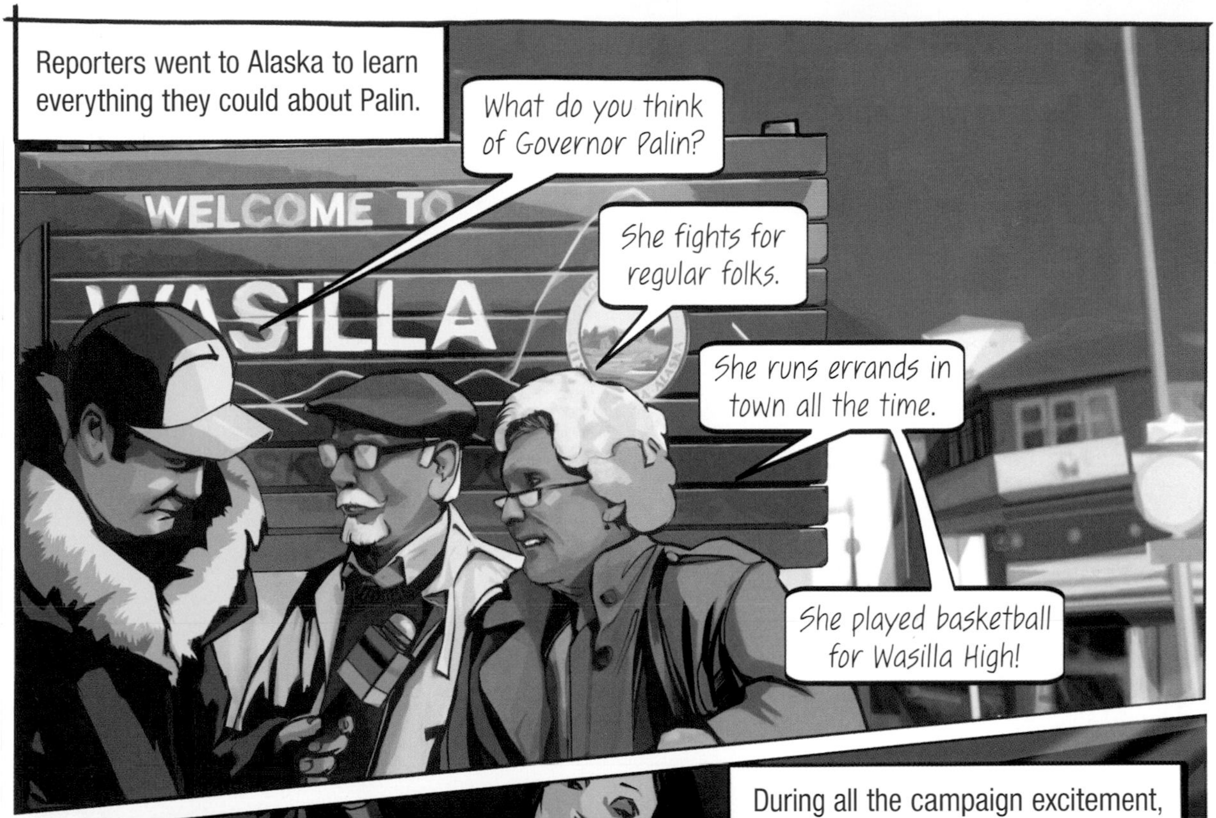
Reporters went to Alaska to learn everything they could about Palin.
What do you think of Governor Palin?
WELCOME TO WASILLA
She fights for regular folks.
She runs errands in town all the time.
She played basketball for Wasilla High!

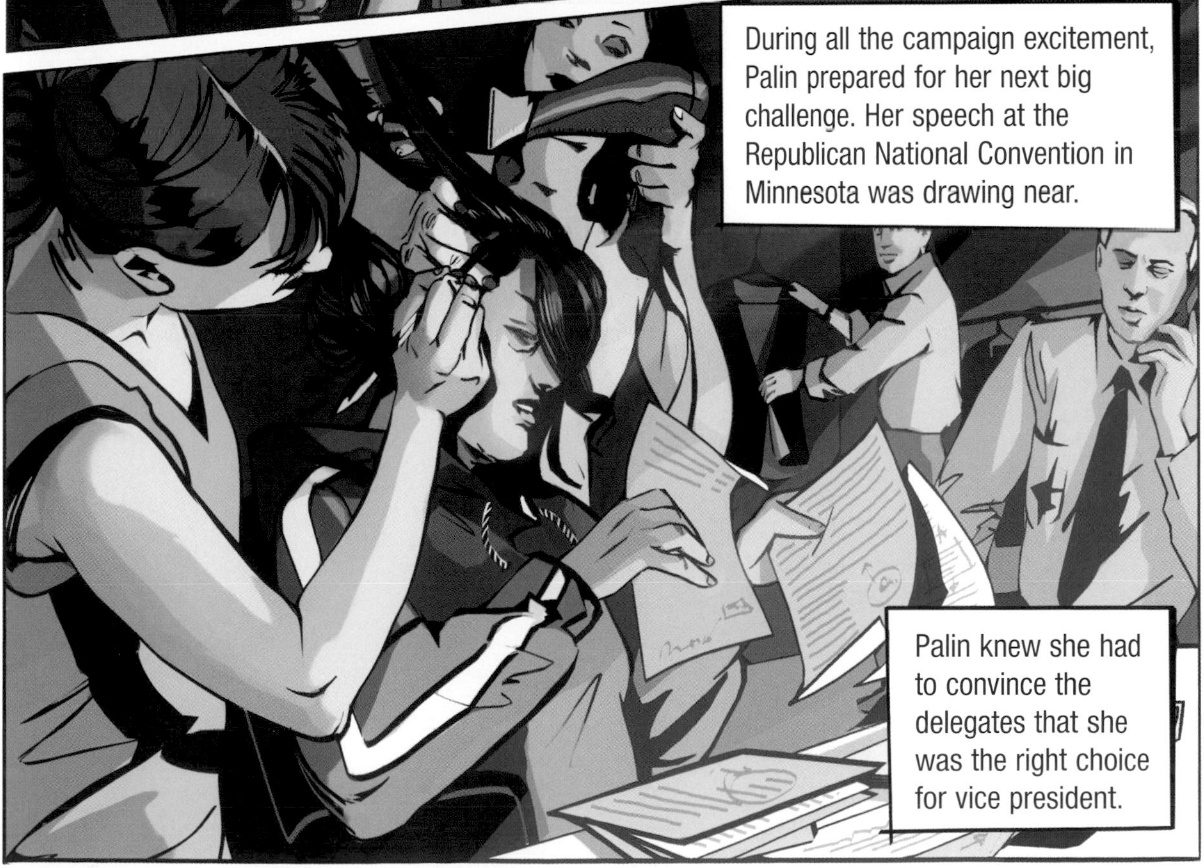
During all the campaign excitement, Palin prepared for her next big challenge. Her speech at the Republican National Convention in Minnesota was drawing near.
Palin knew she had to convince the delegates that she was the right choice for vice president.

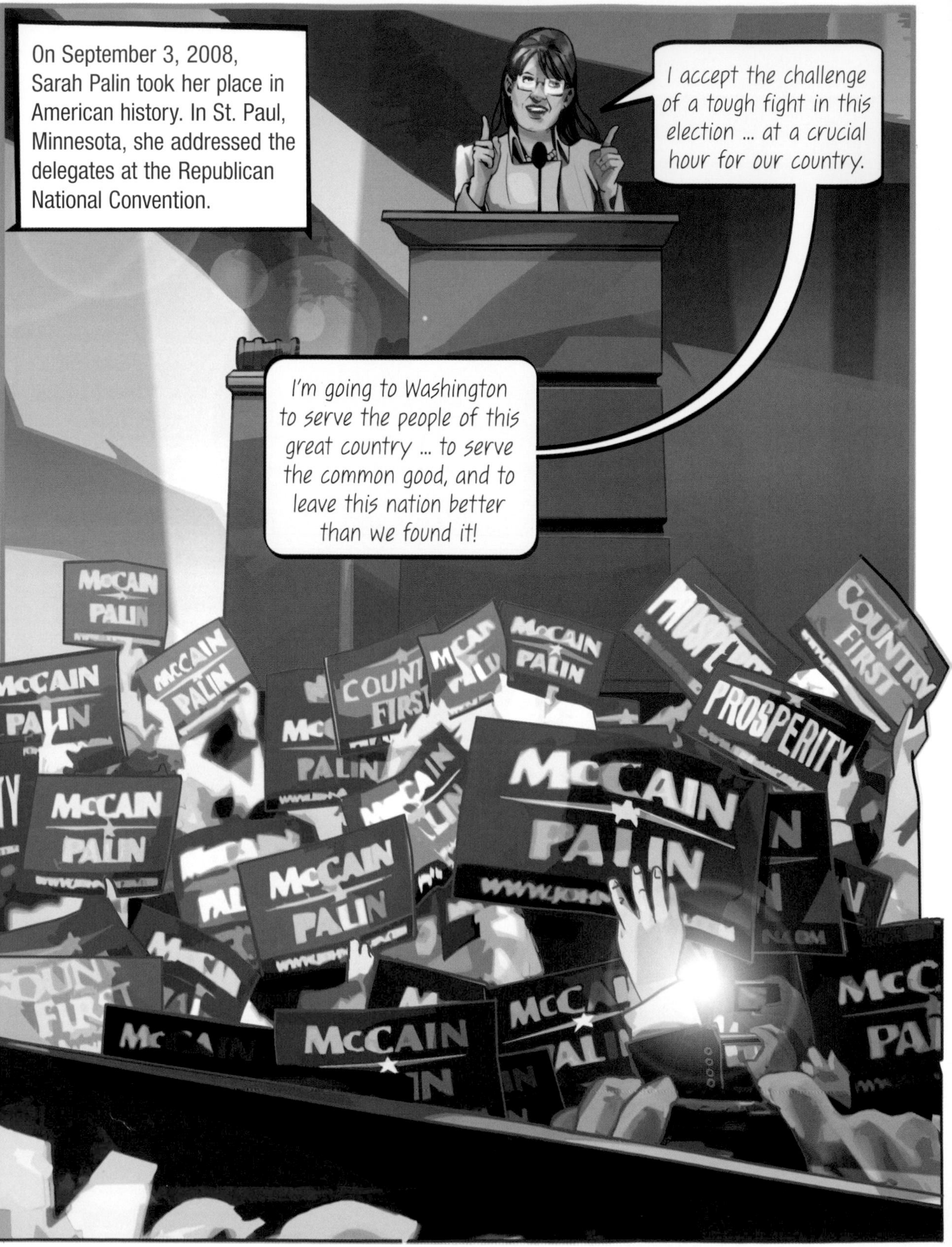
On September 3, 2008, Sarah Palin took her place in American history. In St. Paul, Minnesota, she addressed the delegates at the Republican National Convention.
I accept the challenge of a tough fight in this election ... at a crucial hour for our country.
I'm going to Washington to serve the people of this great country ... to serve the common good, and to leave this nation better than we found it!
McCAIN PALIN
COUNTRY FIRST
PROSPERITY

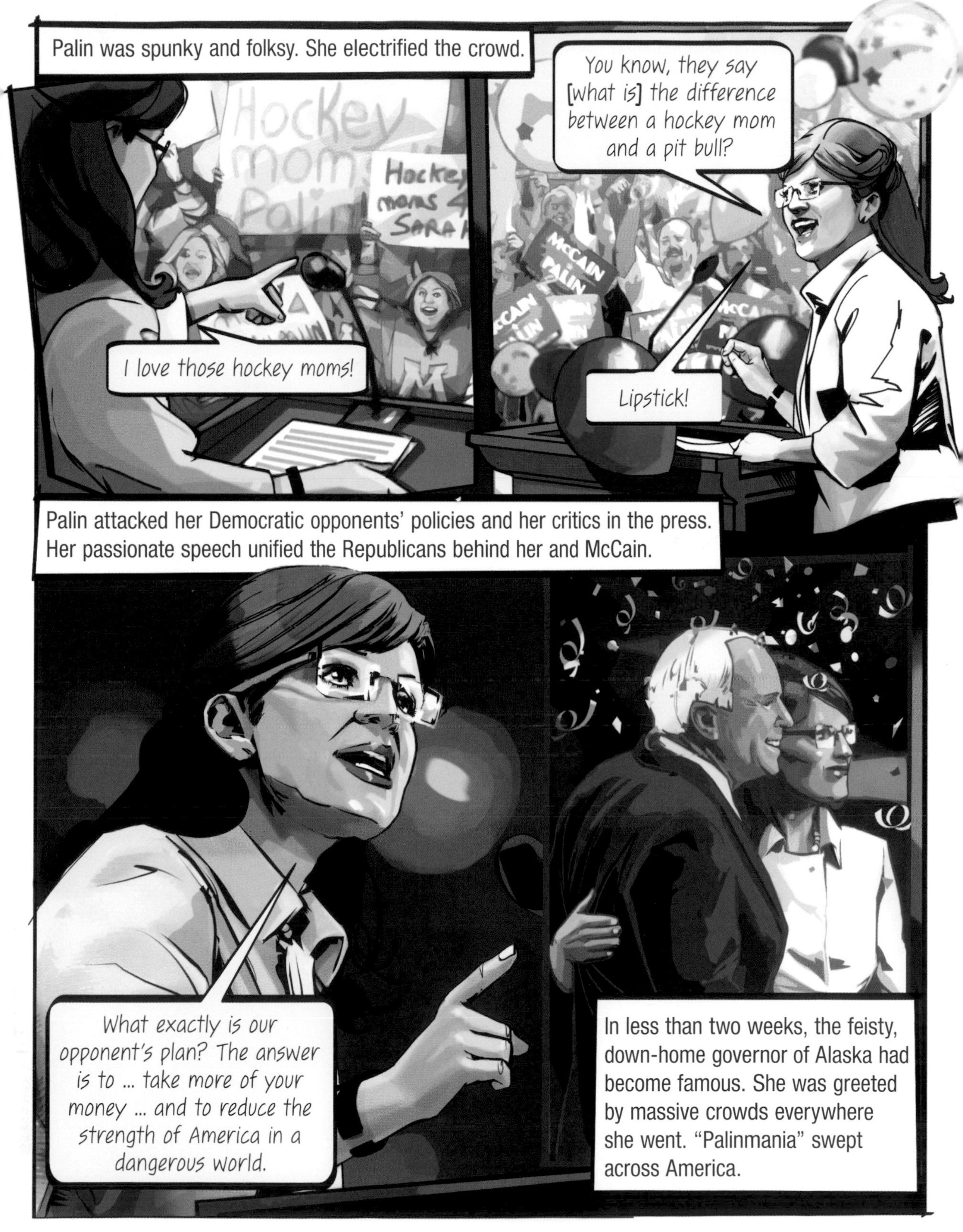

Palin was spunky and folksy. She electrified the crowd.
Hockey moms Palin
I love those hockey moms!
You know, they say [what is] the difference between a hockey mom and a pit bull?
McCAIN PALIN
Lipstick!
Palin attacked her Democratic opponents' policies and her critics in the press. Her passionate speech unified the Republicans behind her and McCain.
What exactly is our opponent's plan? The answer is to ... take more of your money ... and to reduce the strength of America in a dangerous world.
In less than two weeks, the feisty, down-home governor of Alaska had become famous. She was greeted by massive crowds everywhere she went. "Palinmania" swept across America.

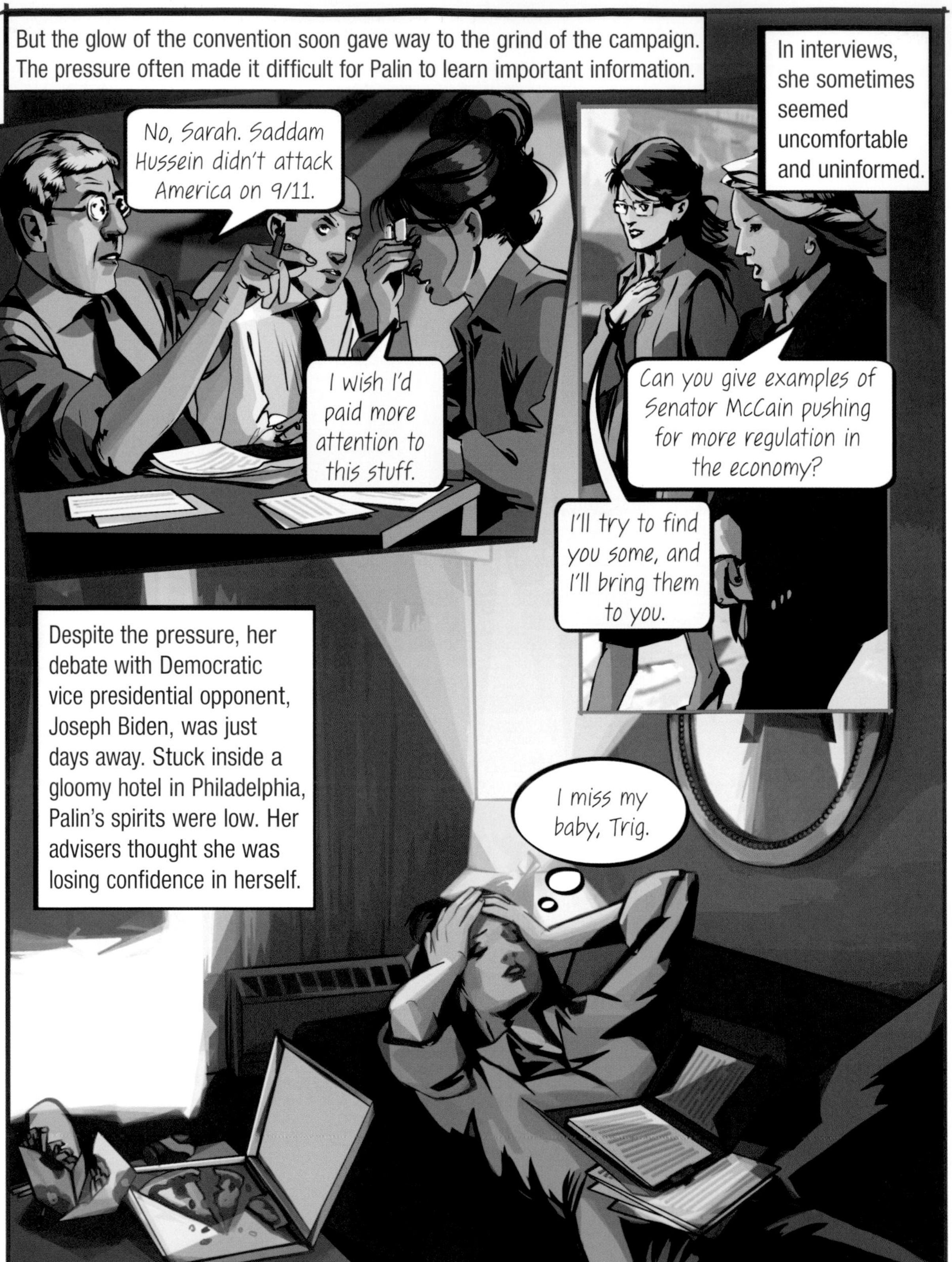
But the glow of the convention soon gave way to the grind of the campaign. The pressure often made it difficult for Palin to learn important information.
No, Sarah. Saddam Hussein didn't attack America on 9/11.
I wish I'd paid more attention to this stuff.
In interviews, she sometimes seemed uncomfortable and uninformed.
Can you give examples of Senator McCain pushing for more regulation in the economy?
I'll try to find you some, and I'll bring them to you.
Despite the pressure, her debate with Democratic vice presidential opponent, Joseph Biden, was just days away. Stuck inside a gloomy hotel in Philadelphia, Palin's spirits were low. Her advisers thought she was losing confidence in herself.
I miss my baby, Trig.

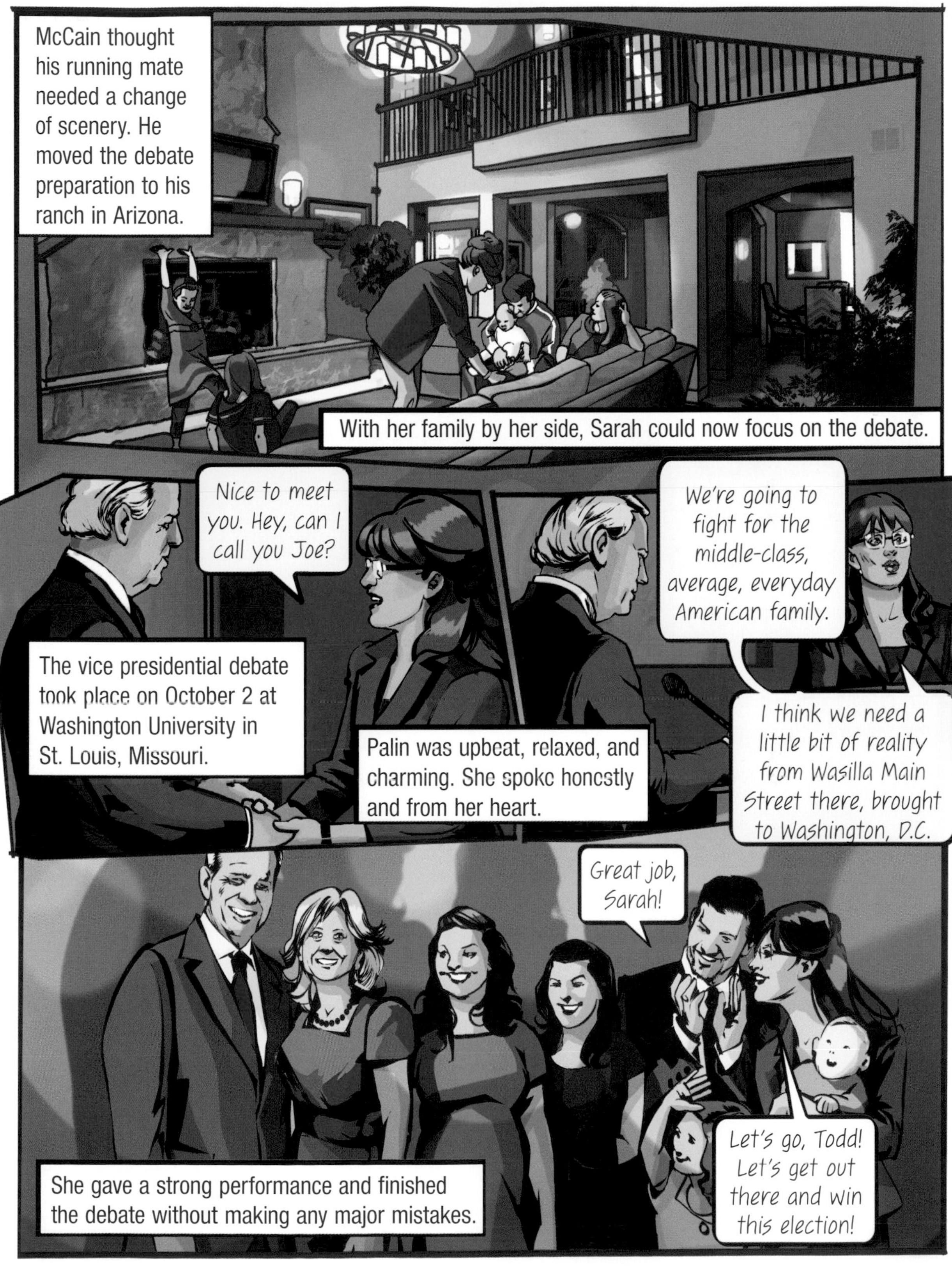
McCain thought his running mate needed a change of scenery. He moved the debate preparation to his ranch in Arizona.
With her family by her side, Sarah could now focus on the debate.
Nice to meet you. Hey, can I call you Joe?
The vice presidential debate took place on October 2 at Washington University in St. Louis, Missouri.
Palin was upbeat, relaxed, and charming. She spoke honestly and from her heart.
We're going to fight for the middle-class, average, everyday American family.
I think we need a little bit of reality from Wasilla Main Street there, brought to Washington, D.C.
Great job, Sarah!
She gave a strong performance and finished the debate without making any major mistakes.
Let's go, Todd! Let's get out there and win this election!

CHAPTER 3
THE VOTERS DECIDE

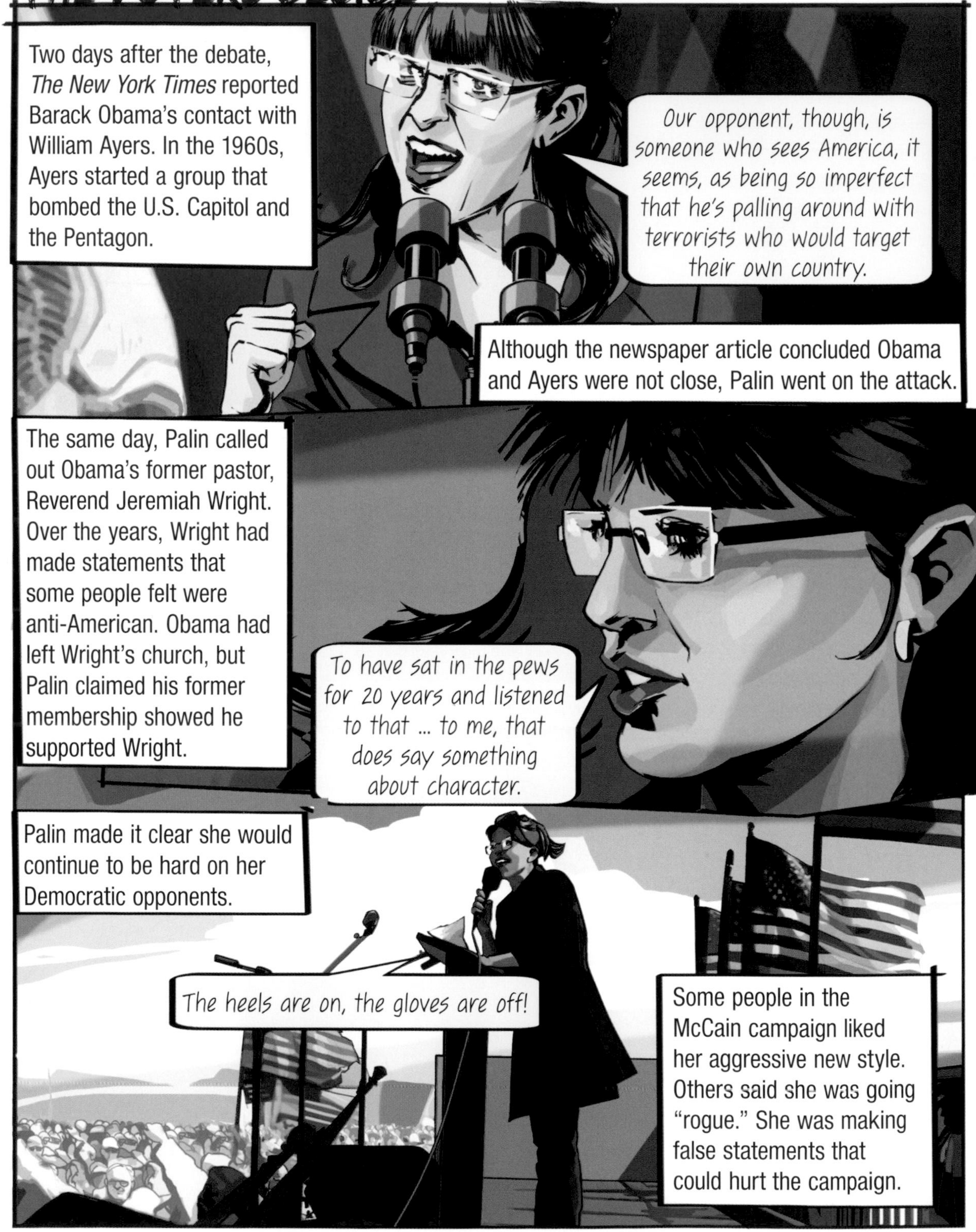

Two days after the debate, *The New York Times* reported Barack Obama's contact with William Ayers. In the 1960s, Ayers started a group that bombed the U.S. Capitol and the Pentagon.
Our opponent, though, is someone who sees America, it seems, as being so imperfect that he's palling around with terrorists who would target their own country.
Although the newspaper article concluded Obama and Ayers were not close, Palin went on the attack.
The same day, Palin called out Obama's former pastor, Reverend Jeremiah Wright. Over the years, Wright had made statements that some people felt were anti-American. Obama had left Wright's church, but Palin claimed his former membership showed he supported Wright.
To have sat in the pews for 20 years and listened to that ... to me, that does say something about character.
Palin made it clear she would continue to be hard on her Democratic opponents.
The heels are on, the gloves are off!
Some people in the McCain campaign liked her aggressive new style. Others said she was going "rogue." She was making false statements that could hurt the campaign.

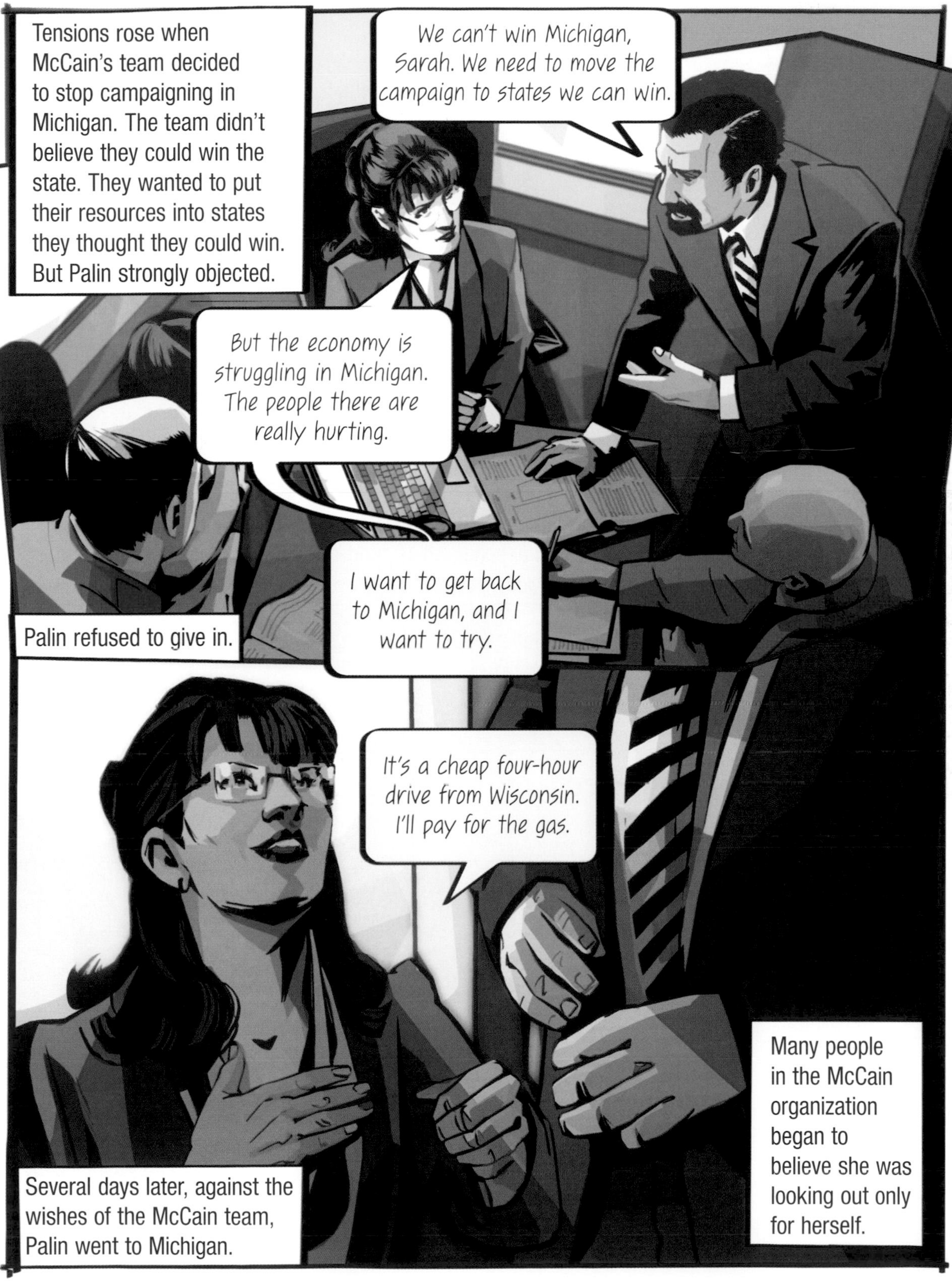
Tensions rose when McCain's team decided to stop campaigning in Michigan. The team didn't believe they could win the state. They wanted to put their resources into states they thought they could win. But Palin strongly objected.
We can't win Michigan, Sarah. We need to move the campaign to states we can win.
But the economy is struggling in Michigan. The people there are really hurting.
Palin refused to give in.
I want to get back to Michigan, and I want to try.
It's a cheap four-hour drive from Wisconsin. I'll pay for the gas.
Several days later, against the wishes of the McCain team, Palin went to Michigan.
Many people in the McCain organization began to believe she was looking out only for herself.

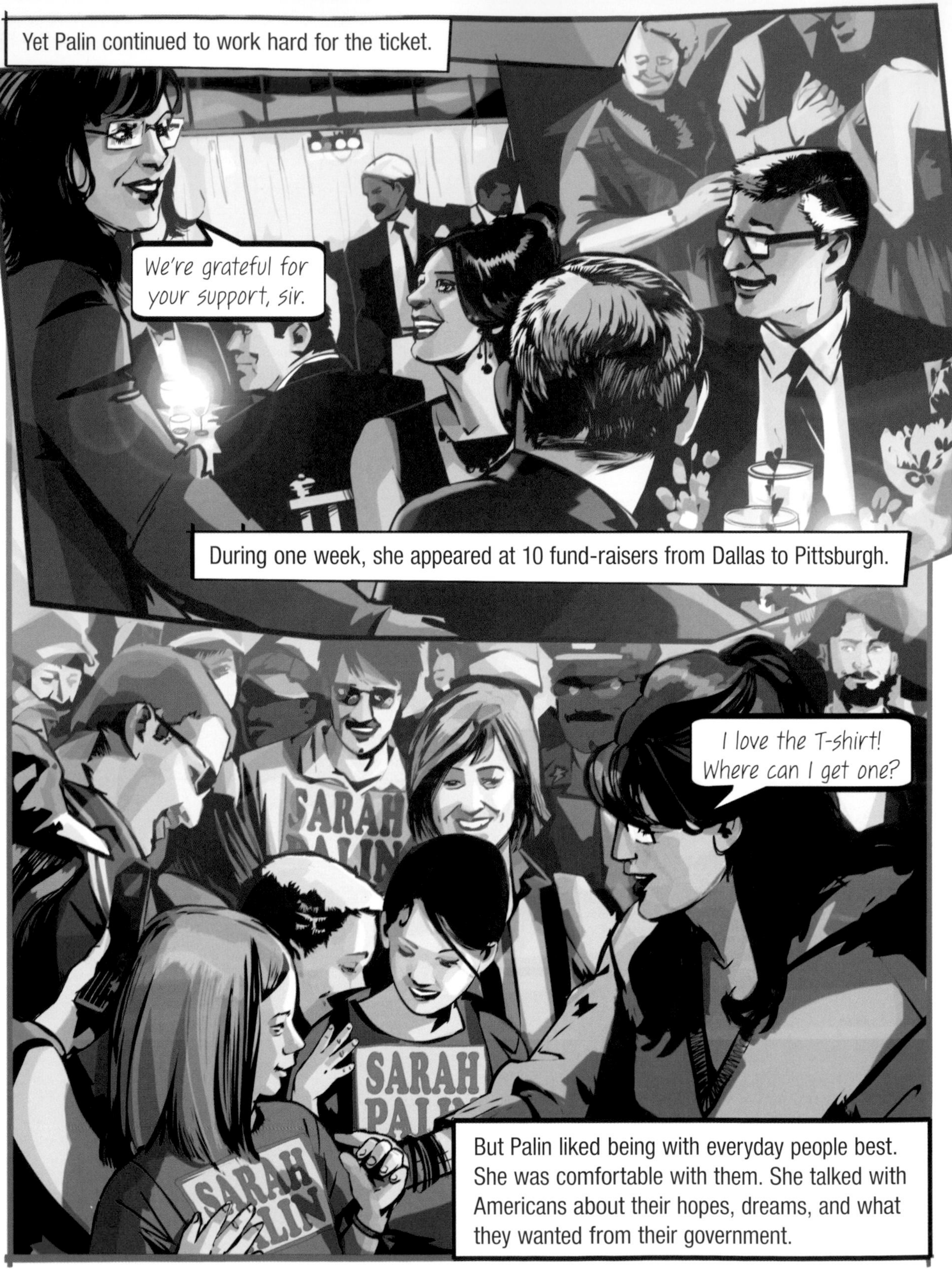
Yet Palin continued to work hard for the ticket.
We're grateful for your support, sir.
During one week, she appeared at 10 fund-raisers from Dallas to Pittsburgh.
SARAH PALIN
I love the T-shirt! Where can I get one?
SARAH PALIN
SARAH PALIN
But Palin liked being with everyday people best. She was comfortable with them. She talked with Americans about their hopes, dreams, and what they wanted from their government.

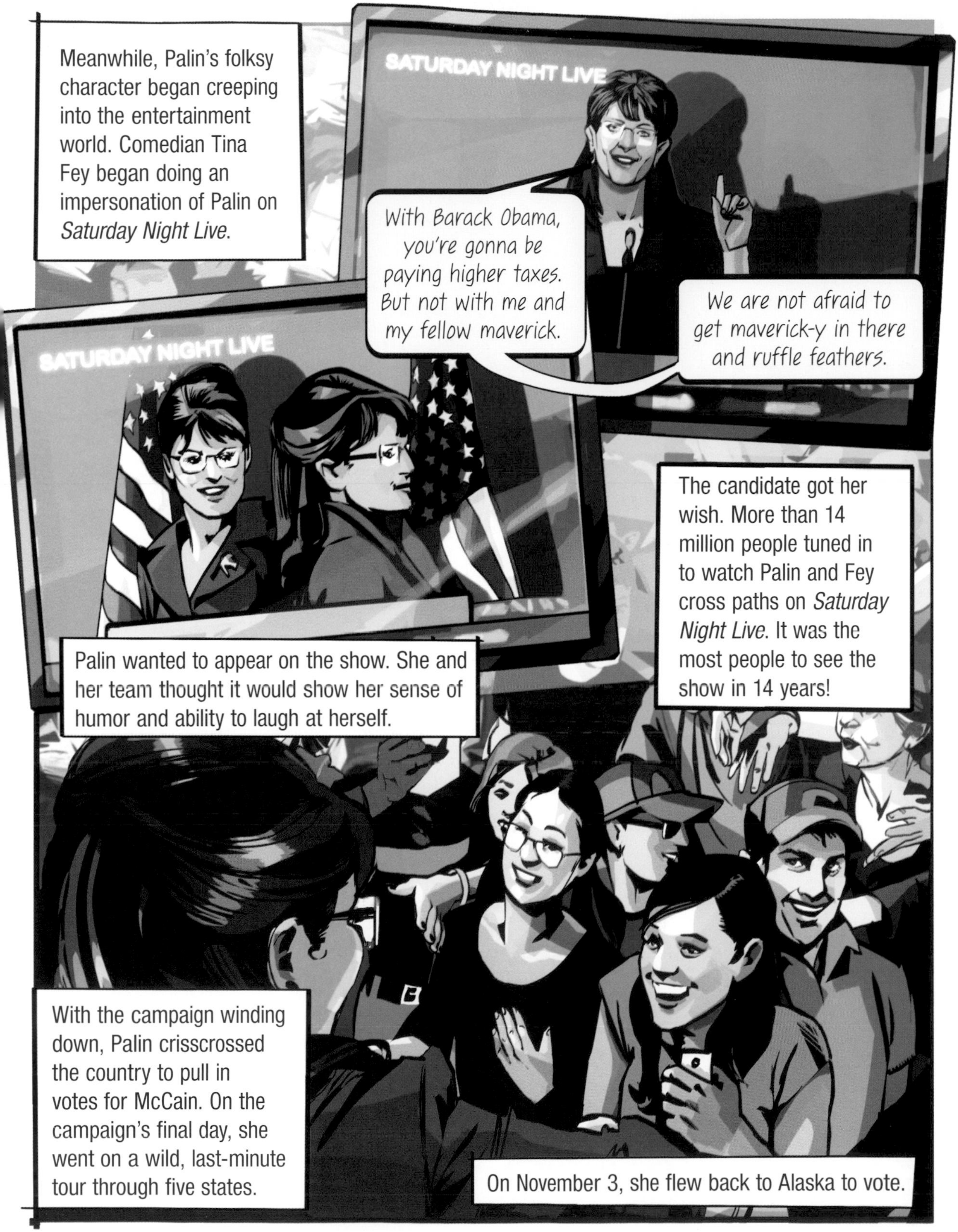

Meanwhile, Palin's folksy character began creeping into the entertainment world. Comedian Tina Fey began doing an impersonation of Palin on *Saturday Night Live*.
SATURDAY NIGHT LIVE
With Barack Obama, you're gonna be paying higher taxes. But not with me and my fellow maverick.
We are not afraid to get maverick-y in there and ruffle feathers.
SATURDAY NIGHT LIVE
Palin wanted to appear on the show. She and her team thought it would show her sense of humor and ability to laugh at herself.
The candidate got her wish. More than 14 million people tuned in to watch Palin and Fey cross paths on *Saturday Night Live*. It was the most people to see the show in 14 years!
With the campaign winding down, Palin crisscrossed the country to pull in votes for McCain. On the campaign's final day, she went on a wild, last-minute tour through five states.
On November 3, she flew back to Alaska to vote.

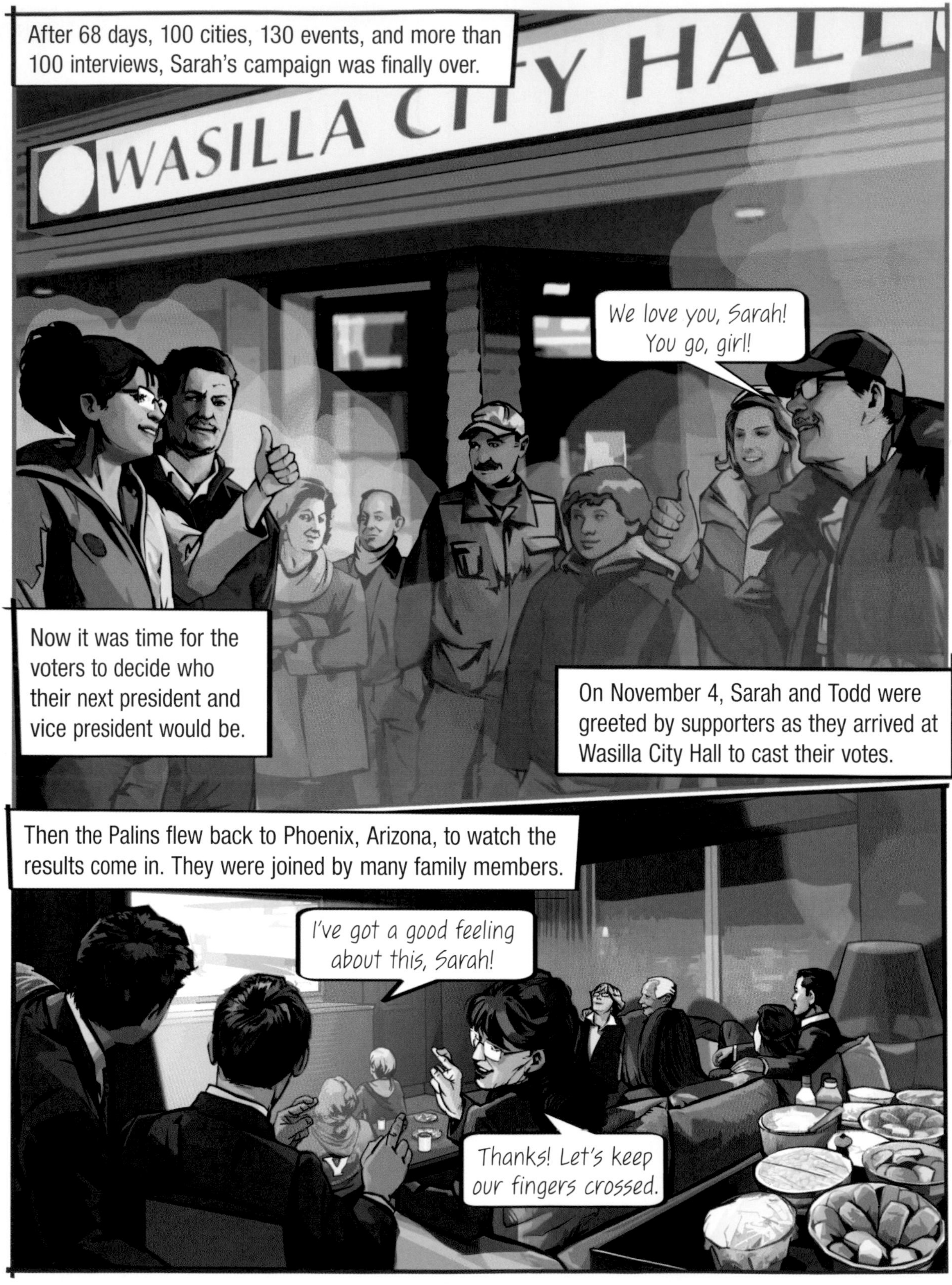
After 68 days, 100 cities, 130 events, and more than 100 interviews, Sarah's campaign was finally over.
WASILLA CITY HALL
We love you, Sarah! You go, girl!
Now it was time for the voters to decide who their next president and vice president would be.
On November 4, Sarah and Todd were greeted by supporters as they arrived at Wasilla City Hall to cast their votes.
Then the Palins flew back to Phoenix, Arizona, to watch the results come in. They were joined by many family members.
I've got a good feeling about this, Sarah!
Thanks! Let's keep our fingers crossed.

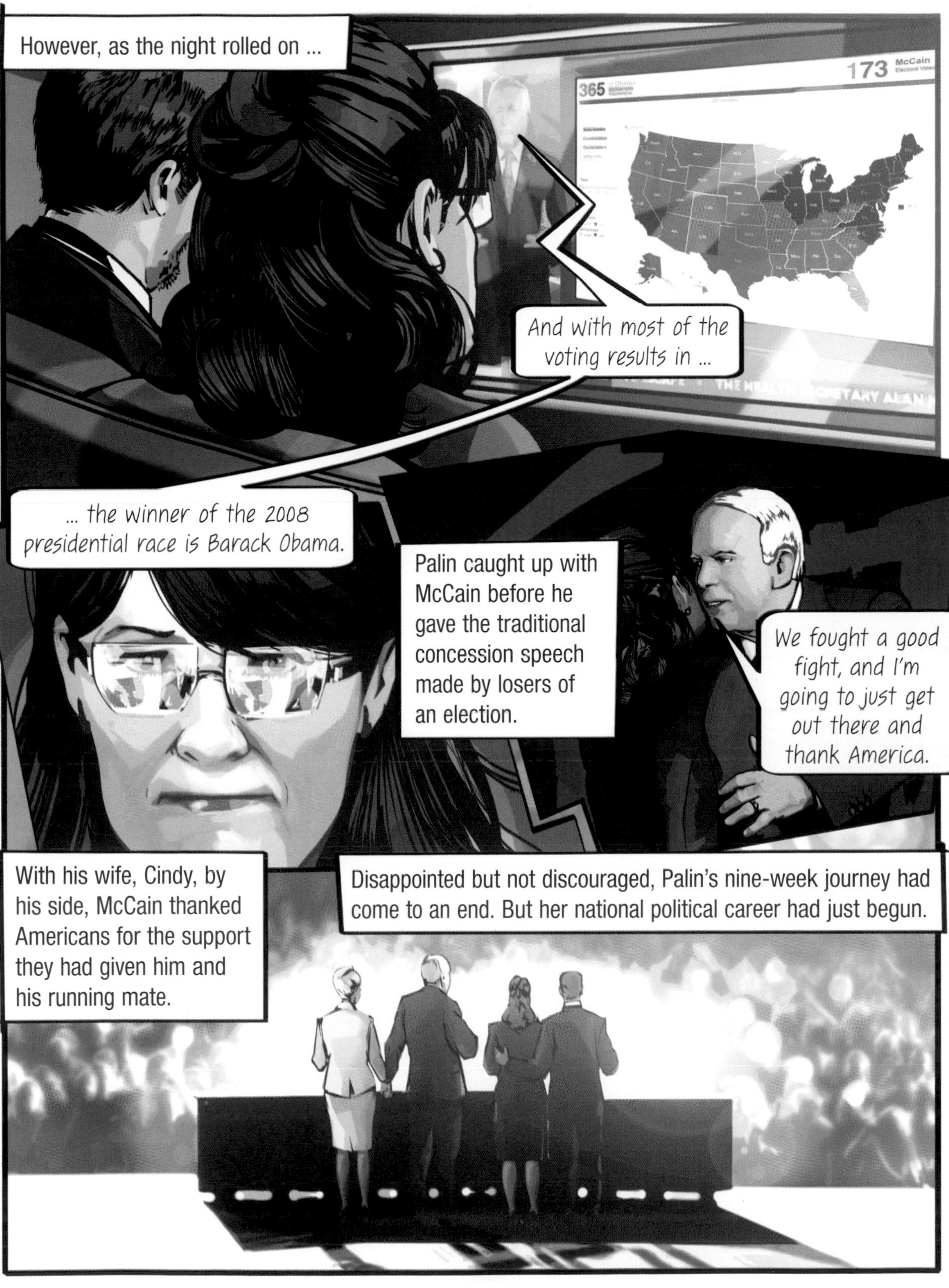
However, as the night rolled on ...
173 McCain Electoral Votes
365 Obama
And with most of the voting results in ...
... the winner of the 2008 presidential race is Barack Obama.
Palin caught up with McCain before he gave the traditional concession speech made by losers of an election.
We fought a good fight, and I'm going to just get out there and thank America.
With his wife, Cindy, by his side, McCain thanked Americans for the support they had given him and his running mate.
Disappointed but not discouraged, Palin's nine-week journey had come to an end. But her national political career had just begun.

CHAPTER 4

NEW BEGINNINGS

After the election, reporters wanted to know if Palin planned to run for president in the future.

If it's good for my family and for the nation, then I might.

FOX NEWS BRE WS

In January 2009, Palin launched a political action committee called SarahPAC. It raised money for state and federal candidates whom she supported.

We will support candidates across the nation who share our hope for reform and positive change.

In only six months, the organization raised $1 million.

But when Palin got back to governing Alaska, some state lawmakers were unhappy. They complained she was ignoring her job in Alaska.

I can't even get her to meet with me.

ALASKA STATE

I know. I keep being told to speak to someone else.

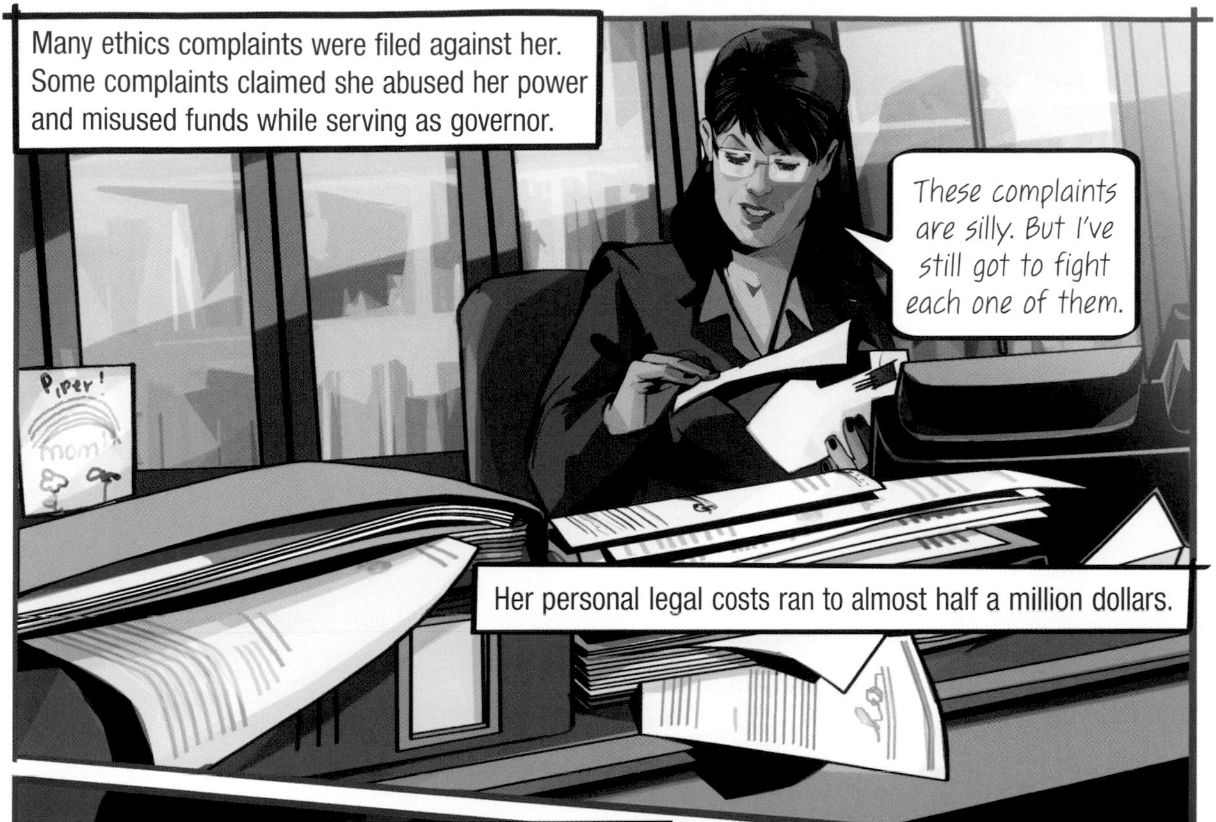
Many ethics complaints were filed against her. Some complaints claimed she abused her power and misused funds while serving as governor.
These complaints are silly. But I've still got to fight each one of them.
Piper!
mom!
Her personal legal costs ran to almost half a million dollars.

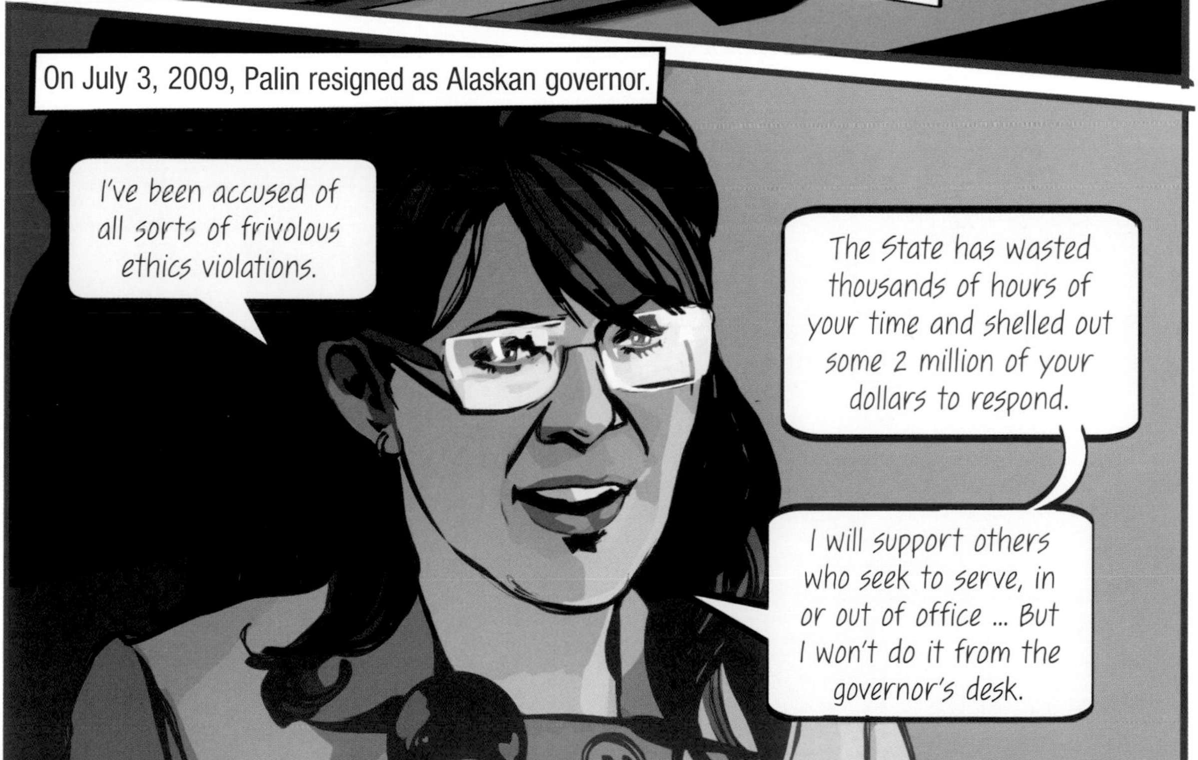
On July 3, 2009, Palin resigned as Alaskan governor.
I've been accused of all sorts of frivolous ethics violations.
The State has wasted thousands of hours of your time and shelled out some 2 million of your dollars to respond.
I will support others who seek to serve, in or out of office ... But I won't do it from the governor's desk.

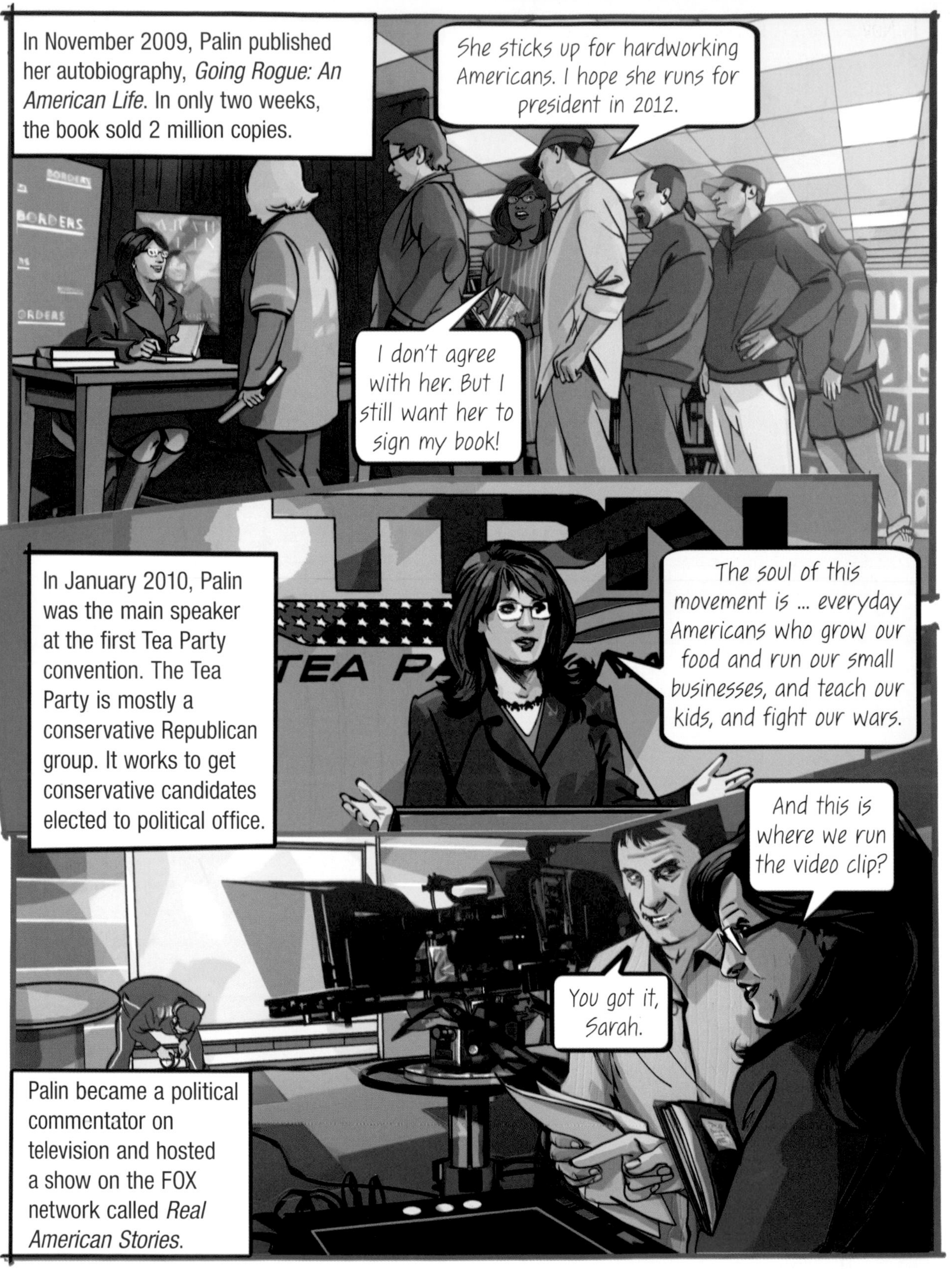
In November 2009, Palin published her autobiography, *Going Rogue: An American Life*. In only two weeks, the book sold 2 million copies.
She sticks up for hardworking Americans. I hope she runs for president in 2012.
BORDERS
I don't agree with her. But I still want her to sign my book!
In January 2010, Palin was the main speaker at the first Tea Party convention. The Tea Party is mostly a conservative Republican group. It works to get conservative candidates elected to political office.
The soul of this movement is ... everyday Americans who grow our food and run our small businesses, and teach our kids, and fight our wars.
And this is where we run the video clip?
You got it, Sarah.
Palin became a political commentator on television and hosted a show on the FOX network called *Real American Stories*.

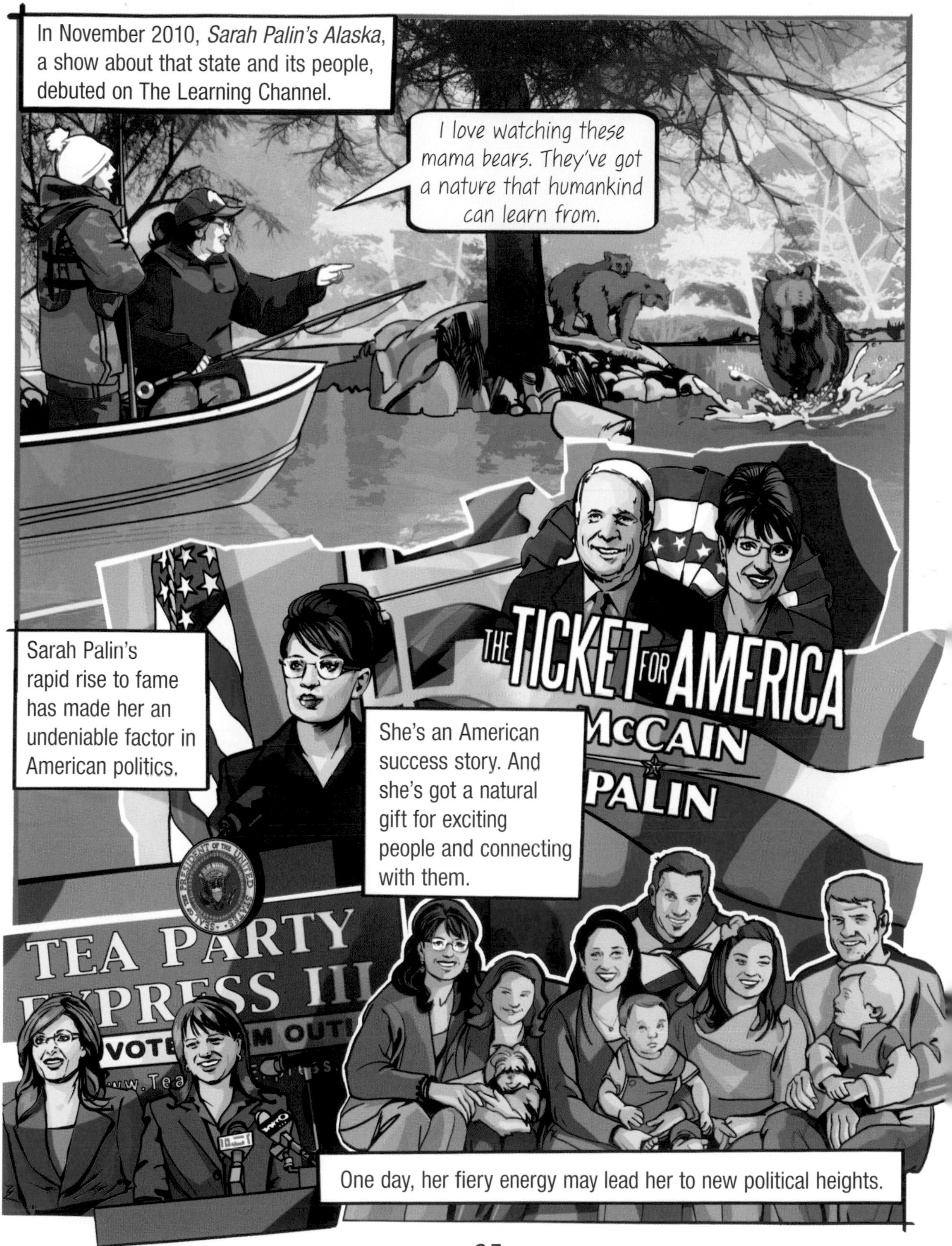
In November 2010, *Sarah Palin's Alaska*, a show about that state and its people, debuted on The Learning Channel.
I love watching these mama bears. They've got a nature that humankind can learn from.
THE TICKET FOR AMERICA
McCAIN
PALIN
Sarah Palin's rapid rise to fame has made her an undeniable factor in American politics.
She's an American success story. And she's got a natural gift for exciting people and connecting with them.
TEA PARTY
One day, her fiery energy may lead her to new political heights.

SARAH FROM ALASKA

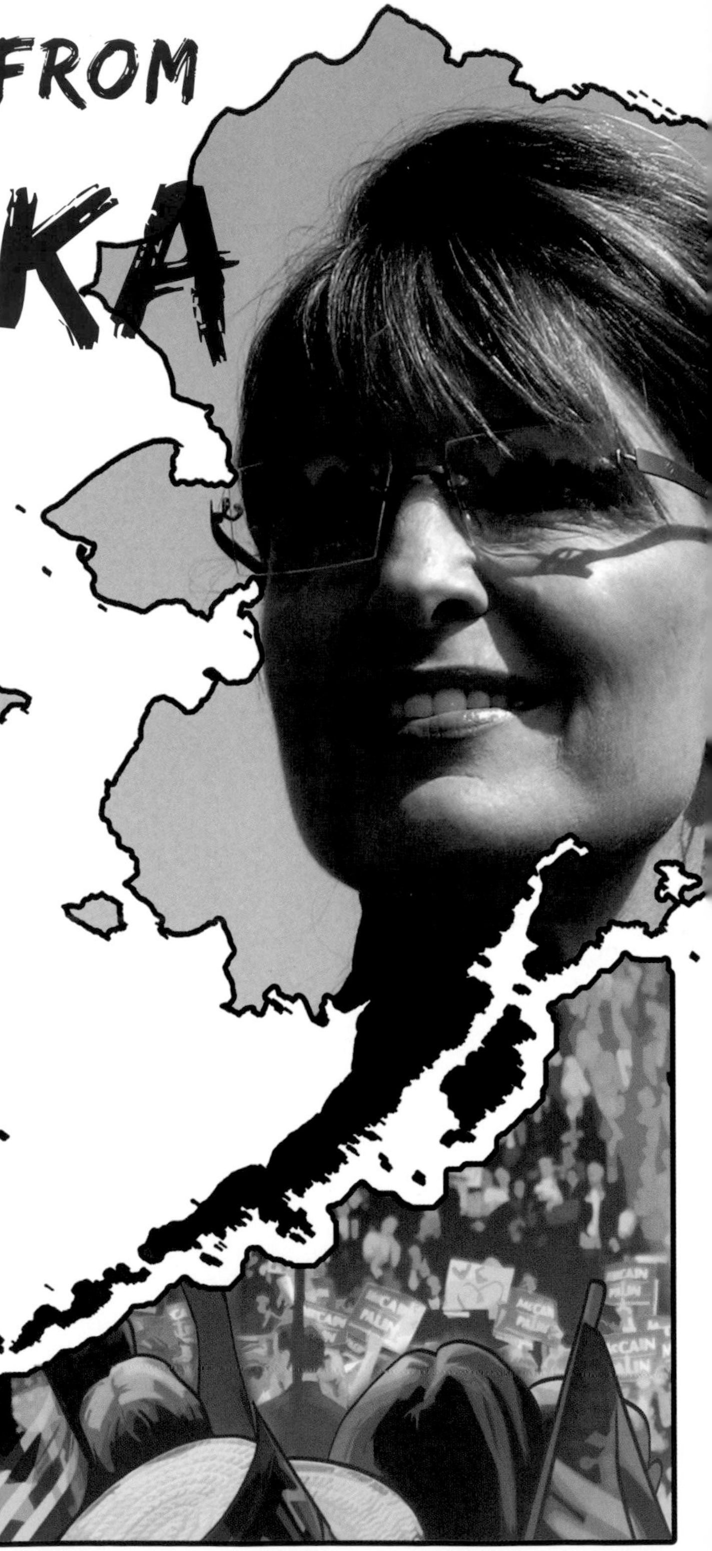

Sarah Louise Palin was born February 11, 1964, in Sandpoint, Idaho. She and her family moved to Alaska in 1966. Palin served on the Wasilla City Council from 1992 to 1996, and was elected mayor of Wasilla in 1996. In 2006 she was elected governor of Alaska. She became Alaska's first female governor. Palin was also the state's youngest governor at age 42. The focus of her administration was oil resource development, education, public health and safety, and transportation.

In August 2008, Palin joined Republican presidential candidate John McCain as his vice presidential running mate. After losing the election in November, she returned to her duties as governor of Alaska. Palin resigned in July 2009.

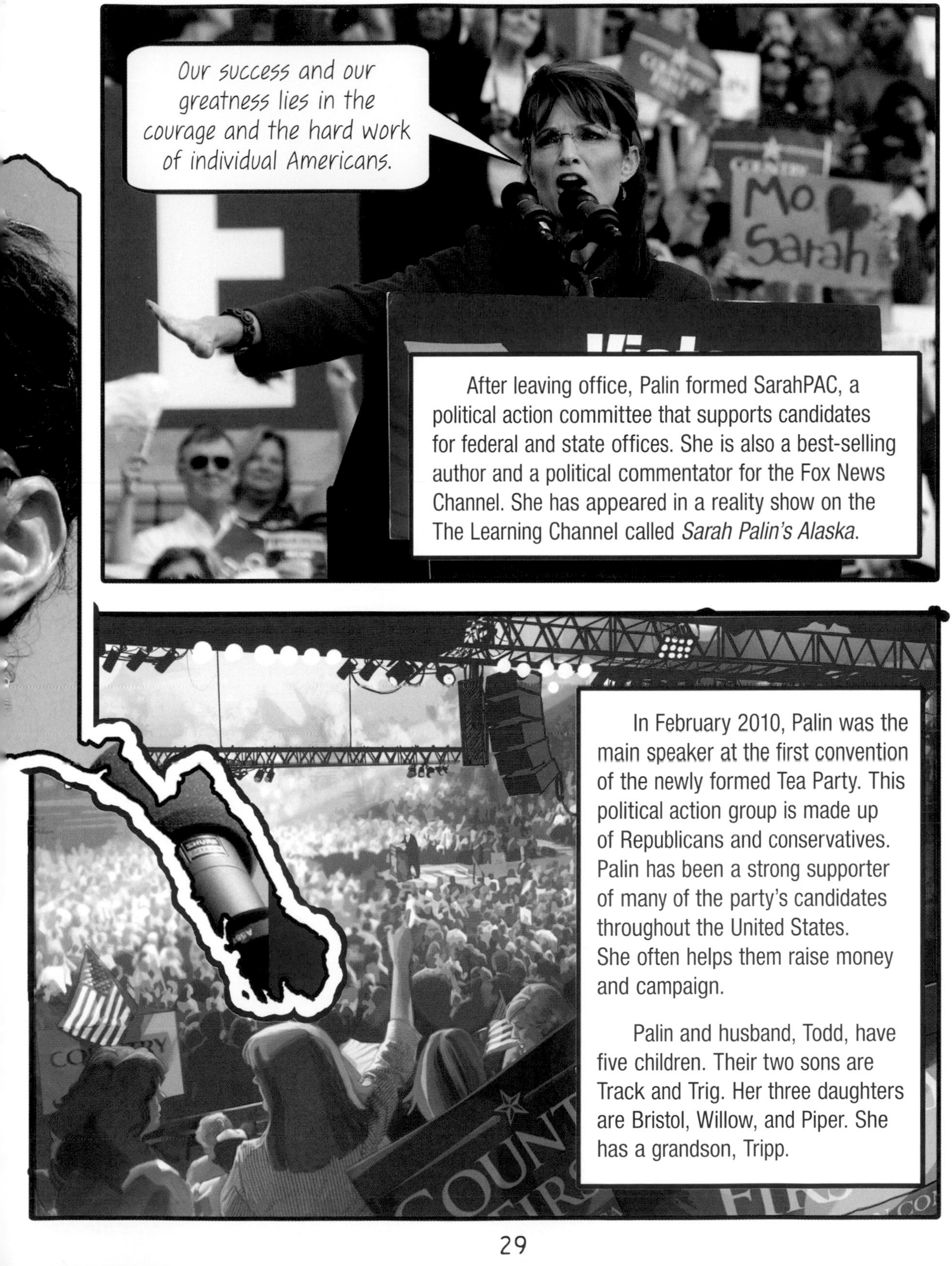
Our success and our greatness lies in the courage and the hard work of individual Americans.
Mo Sarah
After leaving office, Palin formed SarahPAC, a political action committee that supports candidates for federal and state offices. She is also a best-selling author and a political commentator for the Fox News Channel. She has appeared in a reality show on the The Learning Channel called *Sarah Palin's Alaska*.
In February 2010, Palin was the main speaker at the first convention of the newly formed Tea Party. This political action group is made up of Republicans and conservatives. Palin has been a strong supporter of many of the party's candidates throughout the United States. She often helps them raise money and campaign.
Palin and husband, Todd, have five children. Their two sons are Track and Trig. Her three daughters are Bristol, Willow, and Piper. She has a grandson, Tripp.

campaign (kam-PAYN)—organized actions and events with a specific goal, such as being elected

conservative (kuhn-SUR-vuh-tiv)—someone who dislikes change and wants to keep things as they are; in politics, conservatives are said to be on the right

crucial (kroo-SHUHL)—extremely important

delegate (DEL-uh-guht)—someone who represents other people at a meeting

ethics (ETH-iks)—standards of behavior and moral judgment

feisty (FYE-stee)—easily angered or likely to quarrel

impersonation (im-pur-suh-NAY-shuhn)—an act that mimics the characteristics of another person

maverick (MAV-rik)—an independent person who does not go along with a group or a party

poll (POHL)—to count votes; to make a survey

reform (ri-FORM)—to make or bring about social or political changes

reputation (rep-yuh-TAY-shuhn)— a person's character as judged by other people

resolve (ri-ZOLVE)—to decide that you will try hard to do something

rogue (ROHG)—to break away or become uncontrollable

secretive (SEE-kri-tiv)—being silent about something

value (VAL-yoo)—beliefs or ideas that are important to a person

READ MORE

Biskup, Agnieszka. *Obama: The Historic Election of America's 44th President.* American Graphic. Mankato, Minn.: Capstone Press, 2012.

Goldsworthy, Steve. *Sarah Palin.* Remarkable People. New York: Weigl Publishers, 2011.

Petrillo, Lisa. *Political Profiles: Sarah Palin.* Greensboro, N.C.: Morgan Reynolds Pub., 2010.

INTERNET SITES

FactHound offers a safe, fun way to find Internet sites related to this book. All of the sites on FactHound have been researched by our staff.

Here's all you do: Visit *www.facthound.com*

Type in this code: 9781429660181

Super-cool stuff!

Check out projects, games and lots more at
www.capstonekids.com

INDEX

Ayers, William, 18

Biden, Joseph, 16, 17

campaign donations, 12
campaign polls, 4, 12
Culvahouse, A. B., 8

election results, 23

Fey, Tina, 21
fund-raisers, 20

McCain, Cindy, 23
McCain, John, 4, 6, 7, 8–9,
    10, 12, 15, 16, 17, 18,
    19, 21, 23, 28

Obama, Barack, 4, 18, 21, 23

Palin, Bristol, 8, 29
Palin, Sarah
    autobiographies of, 26
    birth of, 28
    family of, 5, 8, 9, 16, 17,
        22, 24, 28, 29
    governorship of, 4, 5, 10,
        12, 15, 24–25, 28
    political views of, 5, 28
    television career of,
        26–27, 29
Palin, Todd, 5, 9, 17, 22, 29
Palin, Trig, 16, 29

Republican National
    Convention, 13, 14–15, 16

Salter, Mark, 6, 7, 8, 9
SarahPAC, 24, 29
Saturday Night Live, 21
Schmidt, Steve, 6, 7, 8, 9

Tea Party, 26, 29

vice presidential debate,
    16, 17

Wasilla, Alaska, 5, 13, 17,
    22, 28
Wright, Jeremiah, 18

AMERICAN GRAPHIC